The tithe is not 10%
IT IS 100%

LAWANDA SCOTT

WESTBOW
PRESS®
A DIVISION OF THOMAS NELSON
& ZONDERVAN

WestBow Press books may be ordered through booksellers or by contacting:

WestBow Press
A Division of Thomas Nelson & Zondervan
1663 Liberty Drive
Bloomington, IN 47403
www.westbowpress.com
844-714-3454

Scripture taken from the King James Version of the Bible.

ISBN: 978-1-6642-7904-9 (sc)
ISBN: 978-1-6642-7903-2 (e)

Print information available on the last page.

WestBow Press rev. date: 12/02/2022

ACKNOWLEDGEMENTS

Thanks be to my heavenly Father and Holy God for his Amazing Grace, and for his calling and choosing me to be a vessel to teach his gospel to many so that he might set captives free through me and that he might be glorified in me, and through me, so that he can make an impact in the world around me.

This book would not have been possible without the encouraging words of support from my two daughters, Kortnea and Dana. I love you both so much.

To My mom, Dora, Thank you for passing to me such a great inheritance of Faith and an example of how to press forward and upward no matter what comes my way. I love you.

CONTENTS

The Tithe is not 10% but 100%--
GIVING- is still required, and are fulfilled by the Holy Spirit, but still required by the Letter.

GIVING- Tithe and offerings, Firstfruits, Redemption Money, Atonement Money are also still required and are fulfilled by the Holy Spirit, but are no longer required by the Letter.

INTRODUCTION

Financial Fulfillment and Freedom- through Grace and Faith in Christ Jesus.

The definition of Fulfillment means to satisfy or meet a requirement fully and completely. Fulfilled does not mean the requirement was abolished or ended. It means it was satisfied. Christ said I did not come to abolish or destroy but to fulfill the law.

Matthew 5:17 Think not that I am come to destroy the law, or the prophets: I am not come to destroy, but to fulfill.

Although, we praise God for our Saviour Jesus Christ for his life, death, and resurrection power over, in and through our lives, I have discovered in the area of Finances we fail to see just how much he has done for us in removing the old ways of the law and its curses, and bringing us under the new covenant of his Grace in our finances. Are you truly ready to be set free in the area of First fruits, Tithe and Offering and Giving, because remember, He whom the Son sets free is free indeed and he desires us to walk in this liberty, this freedom.

John 8:36 If the Son shall make you free, you shall be free indeed

Galatians 5:1 Stand fast therefore in the liberty wherewith Christ hath made us free, and **be not entangled** again with the yoke of bondage.

James 2:10-12 For whosoever shall keep the whole law, and yet offend in one point, he is guilty of all. For he that said, Do not commit adultery, said also, Do not kill. Now if thou commit no adultery, yet if thou kill, thou art become a transgressor of the law.

So speak ye, and so do, as they that shall be judged by the law of liberty.

God has placed in my heart his will to bring us to understanding that the Law of First fruits, the Law Tithe and offering, the Grace Tithe and Offering, and Giving are 4 distinct things. All 4 are required. Yes, that is correct. All 4 are required. However, not in the ways you may be thinking. This is why God wanted this book written.

We must have an understanding of The Law of First Fruits, and Law-Tithe and Offering, (which was the tithe and offering that had to be performed by the letter before Christ), and it's purpose in order to understand the Fulfillment of it By Jesus Christ, our Lord.

God says he desires that we get understanding. He is the one which understanding comes from.

Proverbs 2- The whole chapter, discusses how we are to seek God's knowledge, wisdom and understanding, and how doing so keeps us, protects us, and give us, his children, discernment as we walk in his understanding.

Proverbs 4:5-7 Get wisdom, get understanding: forget it not; neither decline from the words of my mouth. Forsake her not, and she shall preserve thee: love her, and she shall keep thee. Wisdom is the principal thing; therefore get wisdom: and with all thy getting get understanding.

Proverbs 16:16 How much better is it to get wisdom than gold! and to get understanding rather to be chosen than silver!

When we believe in Christ Jesus, and his Holy Spirit abides in us as his child, we now have fulfilled the First fruits and Law Tithe and Offering, and Redemption money, and atonement money, and Passover, and sabbath, and all the law, simply by the Holy Spirit dwelling in our hearts and these carnal ordinances no longer need to be done by the Letter. This Grace -Tithe and offering-which is the fulfillment of the Law of First Fruits and Law Tithe and offering, by the Holy Spirit dwelling in us after we have put our Faith in Jesus Christ. Then after we believe on him, Jesus Christ, who became the First fruits of many, and not a 10 % but a 100% Tithe and the last and final offering forever, we, too have then fulfilled forever in our hearts the Law of First fruits, and Law-Tithe and Offering, and now we come freely to Give, because he has made us free through his Holy Spirit. We therefore give no more grudgingly or out of necessity because of the demands and curses of the Law. We no longer have to give any set percentage by the letter, because Christ has fulfilled it by 100% in the Spirit that dwells in each believer's heart. Those things have been removed by Grace and Faith in Christ Jesus. We set aside each week and bring whatever amount he, God, stirs in our hearts to give, generously and bountifully, because we have already fulfilled the Law and Grace tithe and offering by believing in him. Don't judge another in what is generous or bountiful for them in their different seasons of life. Remember the widow that gave her 2 mites was pleasing to God for he understood it was given generously and bountifully as to how he had blessed her for that time and season of her life. It is not according to man's definition of what is considered generous or bountiful. It is according to what God stirs in the heart of man to give and whatever that is, God considers it generous and bountiful. We can no longer live in man's carnal definition and opinion of spiritual matters. We who are of the Spirit of God must live and walk according to the Spirit mind and word's, not man, because this is what had me in bondage and still have many today in bondage. God is commanding you today, in the name of his Son Jesus Christ, to come out from the places of man's bondages and walk starting today in his liberty. Stop being condemned by man, when God has not condemned you in giving what he places on your heart to give each Sunday, knowing that every Sunday and everyday you as a believer have already fulfilled the tithe.

Matthew 12:7 says

But if ye had known what this meaneth, I will **have** mercy, and **not** sacrifice, ye **would not have condemned the guiltless**.

God was teaching the religious leaders of his day, this principle of not condemning people, saying they are guilty and sinful, when the people they were condemning were guiltless, without guilt, because they were living in grace and liberty through faith and understanding, of what he has fulfilled and done for them, which guarantees the windows of heaven and blessings overflow into our lives forever because we are a believer in Christ Jesus. My giving now is now just heart giving. I am excited and more free in my giving. I don't feel cursed any more, if I am not able to give by the letter 10%, because I understand I have fulfilled the tithe already 100%. I now feel blessed when I give 1%, or 10%, or 30% or 100% of money, because the 100% tithe was fulfilled when I gave my life to Christ. I walk in the liberty of that which Christ has set me free to walk in and of that liberty which he has removed the curse of the law from me by his fulfillment of the law in me through his indwelling of the Holy Spirit. Glory to God. Anybody shouting right there, other than me. Hallelujah to the Lamb of God-Jesus Christ, who is Lord, My Lord and Savior forever. My law Tithe and Offering is fulfillment by the Spirit. My heart stirred free giving is still required to be done, or fulfilled through the letter. It is no longer tied to the law. No one can tell me any longer I am a sinner, or the trials and tribulations I will experience is because the amount I gave this last Sunday was not 10% or above and not considered generous in the church. God said Lawanda if every church member gave 1 million dollars next Sunday, would that be considered generous in society and the church eyes today? I said most definitely. He said I agree. He said this is the thing. Some of those 1 million donations would be only 1% of the person's income, some 10%, some more than 10%, some less than 10%, and some by believers and some by non -believers. Only the believers have fulfilled the tithe. Whether they gave between 1% or 100% of their income does not matter. I desire them to give me themselves first for 100% tithe and offering fulfillment, then to be a generous blessing to others, their church included, by giving what

I lead them to give cheerfully, and that amount is between me and them, and when they obey me, they are my good and faithful servant whom I am well pleased with regardless of what anyone else says. They must walk in this, my approval and my words to them, and stop seeking approval and grace and mercy from men and women of God who I have called and chosen and are being used for my glory, but still are lacking in teaching this important fact of my grace, and who are spewing the wrong rhetoric to my people. This is why I said in Revelation 2 I know the great works they do for me, but nevertheless I have this against them. This is why we must learn from our earthly teachers, through the various resources provided, but must always seek our God in our studies, and learning so we can rightly divide his word and walk in his discernment that we be not deceived by man's misunderstanding of the word or by the devil's temptations to draw us into wrong thinking using the word, as he tried to do with Jesus himself. The devil has no new tricks. Our Godly men and women of God are not the devil, they are men and women who need prayer to be strengthened in their faith in this understanding, that is all. We must stop leaving the faith and our brethren simply because we don't see eye to eye on every issue. This is why God said, pray for one another, restore one another, and he himself, God almighty is able to make each stand. Praying and having healthy conversation and teaching about the bible is our part, bringing understanding and correction in minds and hearts, causing one to stand in the truth, and rightly divide the word, is God alone. In Ezekiel chapter 2 God told Ezekiel he was sending him to a stubborn and rebellious people with his word and Ezekiel was to teach what God told him and not be afraid of the people's faces or their words, and whether the people accepted the words he was teaching or rejected it, was ok, because God told him their blood for their disobedience and rejection of his word was off Ezekiel, because he had obeyed what the Lord had commanded him to do. However, he gave Ezekiel warning also that if he did not do what he commanded him to do and teach what he was sent to give to the people, and the people continued in their ways, then the blood of the people, Ezekiel would be held accountable. Let us all be about our Father's business, not man's any longer. I praise my awesome Father. See he is so good to give us understanding and make it plain.

Just like we are not required to pay atonement money and redemption money by the letter any more as it was under the Law, since Grace through Jesus Christ has come, we are not required to pay 10% Tithe and offering, by the letter, under the law either anymore. They all have been fulfilled by Christ in us 100%.

So, we understand he became our Atonement for our sins. He became our Redeemer, our Passover Lamb, Sabbath, and everything. We now must finally come to understand our Saviour also became our Tithe and offering. 100% tithe and last offering.

This is what this book will help us all to understand and apply the blessed biblical principles God teaches us. Yes, he will stir us to give and we now will give freely whatever he stirs us to give. We must understand the Relationship of Christ to the First Fruits and Tithe Offering and his fulfillment of them through his Body and blood, so that we can walk in the Grace Fulfillment and continually abide there and give freely.

Be blessed as you read this book and learn of him as he teaches His will. Obey his voice and walk in fulfillment and give for the Lord has said:

CHAPTER 1

●

GIVE

Give: (to family, church, friends, charities, community projects, even your enemies-to be a blessing)

God wants to use each of us to be a blessing in giving generously. This area of giving includes a topic of tithing that is quite often a center of debate/discussion/conversation/argument/strife/division. Tithing begin with Abraham when he paid Tithe to King Melchizedek, in honor and worship, gratefulness, and thanksgiving to God for his victory in the war he had just fought. The tithe would later become representative of other things as well, which we will discuss later in the book. For now, read the following scriptures:

Genesis 14:17-20 And the king of Sodom went out to meet him after his return from the slaughter of Chedorlaomer, and of the kings that *were* with him, at the valley of Shaveh, which *is* the king's dale. And Melchizedek king of Salem brought forth bread and wine: and he *was* the priest of the most high God. And he blessed him, and said, Blessed *be* Abram of the most high God, possessor of heaven and earth: And blessed be the most high God, which hath delivered thine enemies into thy hand. **And he gave him tithes of all**.

Tithing would later be instituted as part of the Mosaic law years later as well. Many argue that because tithe and offering begin with Abraham and was before the Mosaic law, this is the reason tithe and offering are to continue by the letter today as instructed. **This is incorrect**.

Circumcision also began with Abraham as we will see in the following scriptures. We also will see that after we have believed in Christ, Circumcision or Non Circumcision by the letter has no value anymore. What matters is that you have believed in Christ and you are a new creation by his Spirit dwelling in you. Which this circumcision now is in the flesh of your heart by the Spirit entering into your heart. This is not the same circumcision required by the letter in the law. They represent the same thing. The old has been satisfied by the new, faith in Christ.

We conclude that just like Christ fulfilled the law and covenant of Circumcision that was given to Abraham, he also fulfilled the law and covenant of Tithe that was given to Abraham. We also know he did become the final offering that was required. Today we are to present ourselves as living sacrifices to him for becoming the final offering that would ever be needed, to cleanse us from our sins. So we have circumcision, tithe, and offering, and all the other Laws fulfilled by –ONE-HIS NAME- JESUS CHRIST. As we believe in him, we are made righteous before our loving God forever for the laws are now fulfilled in us by the Holy Spirit, that we receive by our faith in Jesus Christ.

Read the following:

Genesis 17: 9-10 And God said unto Abraham, Thou shalt keep my covenant therefore, thou, and thy seed after thee in their generations. This *is* my covenant, which ye shall keep, between me and you and thy seed after thee. Every man child among you shall be circumcised.

The law/covenant of circumcision too would become part of the Mosaic Law.

However, after Christ came, he fulfilled the law of tithing, and circumcision, that was began with Abraham as well as all the other Mosaic Laws through grace and our faith to believe in him as Lord and Saviour in our lives for his Holy Spirit to come and dwell in us. This is how the laws are written on our hearts now. This is how the covenant is still being kept forever. This is the new covenant we have with God. **These things no longer are to be done outwardly by the letter. They have been fulfilled by the Spirit. We are circumcised in our flesh not by carnal methods but now by Spirit. We have relationship and covenant with God not by carnal ways but now by the Spirit. We are cut/circumcised in our heart by the Spirit entering in and sealing us forever as his.**

This is why we see Paul saying in:

Galatians 5:2-6 Behold, I Paul say unto you, **that if ye be circumcised, Christ shall profit you nothing. For I testify again to every man that is circumcised, that he is a debtor to do the whole law. Christ is become of no effect unto you, whosoever of you are justified by the law; ye are fallen from grace.** For we through the Spirit wait for the hope of righteousness by faith. **For in Jesus Christ neither circumcision availeth anything, nor uncircumcision; but faith which worketh by love.**

Philippians 3: 3 For we are the circumcision, which worship God in the spirit, and rejoice in Christ Jesus, and have no confidence in the flesh.

★★★Who are the circumcision now according to the above scripture. We are. The believer. The ones that worship God in the Spirit. Those who have believed in Christ, not those who have gotten cut in the flesh but do not believe in Christ. We are. Those who have been circumcised in our heart by the Holy Spirit. In other words, it is no longer a circumcision of the flesh that is needed. It a circumcision of the heart by The Holy Spirit that is required to satisfy the requirements that were under the law.

Therefore, law of tithe and offering and circumcision by the letter have been fulfilled by faith in Christ. Remember he did not come to abolish the laws. He came to fulfill them.

The principle of GIVING is still commanded.

Giving you must still do. Giving money is still required by our Heavenly Father, our holy God, even under the New Covenant. Yes, giving your money as well as your time, gifts, skills, and possessions to be a blessing to others are still required.

We will discuss this in detail as God is leading for he wants to impart understanding to us in this area.

First, let's look at some terms and scriptures that will definitely help in this discussion

Faith: Capacity to believe (in Christ); and to place our trust in one (in Christ)

Read:

Ephesians 2:8 For by grace are ye saved **through faith; and that not of yourselves:** *it is* **the gift of God:**

Grace : Given —something —that we do not deserve-provided to both-Jews and Gentiles —through Christ-alone

We did not deserve his salvation, eternal life, forgiveness, blessings, etc.. But by his grace through Christ we have all this.

Mercy: Not given-something –that we do deserve—provided to both—Jews and Gentiles—through Christ-alone

We deserved to be cursed, condemned, found guilty, because of our sins, but his mercy said no. I set them free, I give them eternal life, salvation, love, forgiveness. I will take their punishment in my own body redeeming them through my own blood. I will nail their sins to the cross forever. I will remove all curses of the law and freely give them all my blessings and make all my promises yes and amen by my Son-Jesus Christ.

Read:

Ephesians 2:1-10 Wherein in time past ye walked according to the course of this world, according to the prince of the power of the air, the spirit that now worketh in the children of disobedience: Among whom also we all had our conversation in times past in the lusts of our flesh, fulfilling the desires of the flesh and of the mind; and were by nature the children of wrath, even as others. **But God, who is rich in mercy**, for his **great love** wherewith he loved us, Even when we were dead in sins, hath quickened us together with Christ, **(by grace ye are saved**;) And hath raised *us* up together, and made *us* sit together in heavenly *places* in Christ Jesus: That in the ages to **come he might shew the exceeding riches of his grace in *his* kindness toward us through Christ Jesus, For by grace are ye saved through faith; and that not of yourselves: *it is* the gift of God: Not of works, lest any man should boast**. For we are his workmanship, created in Christ Jesus unto good works, which God hath before ordained that we should walk in them.

Salvation: delivered from sin and its consequences; preservation from destruction, or the
source or cause of this deliverance or preservation

Saved: to set free from consequences of sin, to rescue from harm or danger, to redeem

We have been delivered, saved, given salvation and eternal life, justified, consecrated, and sanctified, with him and through him, our Lord, Jesus Christ.

Read

1 Thessalonians 5:9–For God hath not appointed us to wrath, but to obtain **salvation** by our Lord Jesus Christ

Eternal life: Life without beginning or end; lasting forever

Read

John 3:36 He that believeth on the Son hath **everlasting life**: and he that believeth not the Son shall not see life; but the wrath of God abideth on him.

Justified: declared or made righteous in the sight of God. Declared in right standing.

Read

Galatians 2:16 Knowing that a man is not justified by the works of the law, but by the faith of Jesus Christ, even we have believed in Jesus Christ, **that we might be justified** by the faith of Christ, and not by the works of the law: for by the works of the law shall no flesh be justified

Consecrated and sanctify means the same thing: to make holy; purify, to set apart for a sacred high purpose.

Read

1 Corinthians 6:9-11 Know ye not that the unrighteous shall not inherit the kingdom of God? Be not deceived: neither fornicators, nor idolaters, nor adulterers, nor effeminate, nor abusers of themselves with mankind, Nor thieves, nor covetous, nor drunkards, nor revilers, nor extortioners, shall inherit the kingdom of God. **And such were some of you: but ye are washed, but ye are sanctified, but ye are justified in the name of the Lord Jesus, and by the Spirit of our God.**

THINGS I'VE LEARNED

CHAPTER 2

LET'S HAVE A LITTLE STUDY ON GENTILES AND JEWS RELATIONSHIP TO MOSAIC LAW

Jews: God's chosen people to whom the Mosaic laws were given to keep them in right standing before God

Gentiles: Anyone not a follower of the true and living God who were considered outcast by the Jews because they were without God and his law.

Mosaic Laws: Laws given by God to Moses for his people to keep in order to have right standing before him. The law was to be their righteousness before God.

Today, Gentile means the man or woman who has not received Christ as their Saviour and therefore cannot be in right standing before God. This man or woman may be Jewish, African American, Chinese, Mexican. Etc. However, when this Gentile receives Christ as Saviour he too becomes one of Christ's chosen/elect, with the righteousness of God abiding forever.

In the biblical days, righteousness to salvation came by the Law. A set of rules, regulations, and carnal ordinances and services that were to be performed **until Christ came** as shown in the scripture below.

Hebrews 9:8-12 The Holy Ghost this signifying, that the way into the holiest of all was not yet made manifest, while as the first tabernacle was yet standing: Which *was* a figure for the time then present, in which were offered both gifts and sacrifices, that could not make him that did the service perfect, as pertaining to the conscience; *Which stood* only in meats and drinks, and divers washings, and carnal ordinances, **imposed** *on* **them** **until the time of reformation.** **But Christ being come** an high priest of good things to come, by a greater and more perfect tabernacle, not made with hands, that is to say, not of this building; Neither by the blood of goats and calves, but by his own blood he entered in once into the holy place, having obtained eternal redemption *for us*

Galatians 3:24-25 Wherefore the **law was our schoolmaster** *to bring us* **unto Christ**, that we might be justified by faith. **But after that faith is come, we are no longer under a schoolmaster.**

Many of the carnal ordinances included being circumcised, observing Sabbath days and Sabbath years, various other festivals such as the Passover, Feast of Tabernacles and Feast of Booths, Tithing and offerings of grains, herbs, and animals, blood sacrifices, various washings, and the refraining from eating certain meats. There were other civil and moral parts of the law that still dealt with walking in love with one another such as thou shall not kill, steal, commit adultery, you should have no other god before God, you should honor your mother and father etc. were all part of the Law. The Law was the way for the people to be holy before a holy God. Now Christ has come to make us holy before our Holy God, forever. That even when we commit a moral sin, which God, does not desire for anyone to sin, but if we do fail and yield to the flesh rather than the Spirit, as a believer, he does not condemn us, but is faithful and just to forgive us, if we repent, confess and ask for his forgiveness.

He told the Jews that he was the **<u>fulfillment of the law</u>** and anyone who now wanted to be in right standing, justified, sanctified and consecrated before God and receive salvation and eternal life had to now do -**one thing -believe in Him.**

Salvation, and Righteousness/Right standing before God forever/and Eternal Life- now came by Christ alone.

Not only Salvation, but continuous right standing with God after Salvation, came by faith in-Christ alone. No longer by the performance of works of the law. This does not mean we were not to still do good works towards one another. Brotherly love was to continue. We were to still do good works and walk in love.

Faith without works is dead. We are justified before man by our works, but never before God does our works justify us, it is only by faith alone are we justified before God. God will still bless us according to our faith when we do good works, and he will chastise us if we need it, and have mercy as well. However, because in any given day we may do 200 good works and 5 bad or 200 bad works and 5 good, just hypothetical, we must remember we still have broken the laws of God. He is the God that said if you have broken one law you have broken them all, because he is the same God that said do not commit adultery that also said do not steal or lie. Since none of us are just that perfect to keep all the laws at the same time by the letter, we give glory to God for fulfillment of the law in us completely, by the Spirit, because although we are in the Spirit we are still in the flesh body, in which we sometimes fall short and sin in this body. Thanks be to God there is no condemnation to those who are in Christ Jesus.

This is why Paul said, Thanks be to God for Jesus Christ. That is why God sent his Son, the perfect lamb, the perfect Saviour to remove this sin stain forever from us through the fulfillment of all the laws through the Holy Spirit. We praise God that we are now hid in Christ Jesus so when we mess up, our heavenly Father sees the blood of Jesus over our lives and extends to us his mercy and grace to get up with another chance to get it right, and this grace and mercy sometimes does still come with suffering the consequences for our action as chastisement from our Father. It is still grace and mercy and another chance to get it right, nevertheless. Own it, correct it, learn from it, and arise from it.

So now when we perform our bad works, in spite of the good works within the day, he looks at Jesus, for we are hid in Christ, by our faith in Christ.

Therefore, God in his mercy, grace and compassion sends the blessings and promise he promised to us based not on the works of our day to day living, but based on the Faith in our Lord and Saviour Jesus. This is why we read scriptures that he says, let it be done to you according to your Faith. You can say, yes, if I sow, and give, and be obedient and keep the commandments he will bless me in my deeds, in my works, but it is not just based on the one actual deed, because I miss it on other good deeds even when I do the one, so it has to still be based not on my works but only according to my Faith in Christ, because if he looked at all our deeds, works, he would see a mixture of good and bad works day to day, and we would qualify for NOTHING, not one blessing, not one promise to be given to us, however thanks be to God for GRACE, he looks at our Faith (in Jesus), and says according to your faith be it done unto you, and be of good comfort, thy faith hath made thee whole, continue to good works for faith without works is dead. I tell you. It is good to know Our Father God is the same yesterday, today, and forever, for every situation of our lives. Our Faith in Christ is powerful to make us whole where we have become sick and broken in even our Finances.

Read the following:

Matthew 9:29
Then touched he their eyes, saying, According to your faith be it unto you

Matthew 9:22 But Jesus turned him about, and when he saw her, he said, Daughter, be of good comfort; thy faith hath made thee whole. And the woman was made whole from that hour.
Read the following:

We know we are to do good works and there is blessings and rewards in doing good works, not an argument, but remember the following scripture as well.

James 2:10-12 For whosoever shall keep the whole law, and yet offend in one *point*, he is guilty of all. For he that said, Do not commit adultery, said also, Do not kill. Now if thou commit no adultery, yet if thou kill, thou art become a transgressor of the law. So speak ye, and so do, as they that shall be judged by the law of liberty.

Conclusion: Yes. We must have faith in Christ. Yes. We must do good works along with having faith. Yes. We are blessed for doing the good works in Faith. However, if we break one law God says we have broken them all. Therefore he made the blessings come because of the FAITH, NOT BECAUSE OF THE WORKS, which mean the blessings and promises are no more by our WORKS but only by GRACE and FAITH. We still must maintain good works, always. Our works show to the world we are followers of Christ. We are justified in man's eyes as followers of Christ by the works they see us do. We are justified only by our Faith in God's eyes. We have not been given license to sin. Glory to God. We should remember, it is because of our Faith in Jesus that we get the promises and the blessings and not the curses. It is because of this same grace and faith that we, even do the good works.

THINGS I'VE LEARNED

CHAPTER 3

MAINTAINING GOOD WORKS IS OUR REASONABLE SERVICE UNTO THE LORD

Read the following:

Romans 12:1 I beseech you therefore, brethren, by the mercies of God, that ye present your bodies a living sacrifice, holy, acceptable unto God, *which is* your reasonable service.

As a believer, we are not perfect as we walk in this flesh. It is still a tug a war between our carnal/flesh and Spirit daily. We lose the battle sometimes. We all do. We miss the mark in breaking a law daily, intentionally or unintentionally. We praise and give all thanks and glory to God for hiding us and our sinful state in Christ. We give him praise for giving us through Christ the opportunity to confess and repent of our sins. God does not want any of us to sin, but he knows the war we deal with daily, because he too became Spirit wrapped in flesh as we are, and he therefore now has given us his Son as our Advocate. We have the perfect one dwelling in us, and interceding for us, if we are a believer, and we are hid in him.

Read the following:

Colossians 3:3 For ye are dead, and your life is hid with Christ in God.

Thank God, for Christ. By Christ we have GRACE. This Grace, causes God to look past my sins in the flesh to the Spirit of Christ in me and his blood over my life as I go boldly to the throne of grace seeking his mercy so I can find grace in my time of need, EVERYTIME, as I confess, repent and ask my loving Father for forgiveness.

Are we justified by faith alone or are we justified by works with our faith? He said we must show we love him or we are not of him, right? These questions have caused so much confusion. God wants to give understanding.

Read the following scriptures:

These two scriptures tells us we are not justified by the works of the law but by faith only.
Galatians 2:16 Knowing that a man is not justified by the works of the law, but by the faith of Jesus Christ, even we have believed in Jesus Christ, that we might be justified by the faith of Christ, and not by the works of the law: for by the works of the law shall no flesh be justified.

Romans 3:20-23 Therefore by the deeds of the law there shall no flesh be justified in his sight: for by the law *is* the knowledge of sin. But now the righteousness of God without the law is manifested, being witnessed by the law and the prophets; Even the righteousness of God *which is* by faith of Jesus Christ unto all and upon all them that believe: for there is no difference: For all have sinned, and come short of the glory of God

Then these scripture tells us we are not justified by faith only. Faith without works is dead.

James 2:17-24 Even so faith, if it hath not works, is dead, being alone.Yea, a man may say, Thou hast faith, and I have works: shew me thy faith without thy works, and I will shew thee my faith by my works. Thou believest that there is one God; thou doest well: the devils also believe, and tremble. But wilt thou know, O vain man, that faith without works is dead? Was not Abraham our father justified by works, when he had offered Isaac his son upon the altar? Seest thou how faith wrought with his works, and by works was faith made perfect? And the scripture was fulfilled which saith, Abraham believed God, and it was imputed unto him for righteousness: and he was called the Friend of God. Ye see then how that by works a man is justified, and not by faith only. Likewise also was not Rahab the harlot justified by works, when she had received the messengers, and had sent *them out* another way? For as the body without the spirit is dead, so faith without works is dead also.

John 14:15 If ye love me, keep my commandments.

John 14:21 He that hath my commandments, and keepeth them, he it is that loveth me: and he that loveth me shall be loved of my Father, and I will love him, and will manifest myself to him.

So, which is it? BOTH. Yes. Both. In the first 2 scriptures where God talks about no flesh is justified by works talks about before HIM- God. We can never do enough good works to be justified before him. Only Jesus' Righteousness does that for us.

So why do we have to do good works along with faith in Jesus? So, we can be justified before MAN that we are followers/disciples of Jesus. Our works show others that we are believers in Jesus our Lord. We are justified by our works that we love him and follow and obey the things he tells us to do. However, in our day to day living we still fall short in doing everything just right. We don't always forgive as we should. We don't always love and have compassion as we should. This is why we do fall short at times in being justified before MAN, but never being Justified before GOD because of Jesus. Yes, we are to do good works so others will see the Lord living in us. However, all the promises and blessings are manifested to us because of the goodness of God when we confessed him as Lord and Saviour of our lives, he then gave us all that was his, not because of the daily works.

This is why it is important for us to understand the difference between these scriptures, so we will not continue to allow the enemy to pit us against one another with the use of these scriptures, or to put the believer in condemnation as he has been so readily doing successfully. Take back your liberty and your victory and justified status in Jesus Christ. Stand boldly therein.

Live in freedom in knowing you are always justified before God without works and his grace and mercy will help you always because of Jesus, even if it is simply giving us the strength and perseverance to endure our punishments and consequences of some of our actions, or to do his will as Jesus, Job, and Stephen were called to do. Suffering for doing right. God is faithful, even when we are not justified before man sometimes due to our short comings in doing the works of the law as commanded, but we are always justified before God by faith alone. We are to strive to do right everyday and not sin. It is hard. God is here with us always to help us fight the good fight of faith. Keep your hand in his.

This is why we are not justified before God by our works of the law:

Broken One –Broken All

James 2:9-12 But if ye have respect to persons, ye commit sin, and are convinced of the law as transgressors. **For whosoever shall keep the whole law, and yet offend in one *point*, he is guilty of all.** For he that said, Do not commit adultery, said also, Do not kill. Now if thou commit no adultery, yet if thou kill, thou art become a transgressor of the law. **So speak ye, and so do, as they that shall be judged by the law of liberty.**

2 Corinthians 1:20 For all the promises of God in him *are* yea, and in him Amen, unto the glory of God by us.

If you are living by the law, you know that scripture Malachi that we use so very often to condemn those who do not pay a tithe by the letter, because we do not understand the tithe that was by the letter has been fulfilled by the Spirit by Grace and is no longer required by the letter. Every day I have the Spirit in me. Every day my tithe has been fulfilled.

Malachi 3:10 Bring ye all the tithes into the storehouse, that there may be meat in mine house, and prove me now herewith, saith the LORD of hosts, if I will not open you the windows of heaven, and pour you out a blessing, that *there shall* not *be room* enough *to receive it.*

Now, let's look at this scripture of Malachi connected with the James and Galatians scripture. The meaning of these scriptures in the following example is:

I'm a tither but I also have respect to persons, tither but a murder, tither but a bank robber, tither but a drug dealer, tither but a woman abuser, liar, and if none of these got you, well I say to you like Jesus, you still lack one thing, you insert one of your own shortcomings here that you know you have but the world does not know you have or see. See none of us, what God is revealing, can ever keep every law perfectly one by one to equal them as wholly and completely done and satisfied in ourselves. We all always fall short in one or the other. This is why he reminds us like he did the young ruler. What is impossible for man to do for himself according to his works of the law is possible with Jesus alone. We will never be justified before our heavenly father by our Works. There was a man in the bible possessed by Legions of demons, and Jesus was able to deliver him and set him in his right mind. He is the same today. Delivering each of us from whatever the Legion is, i.e whatever the sin or evil that is so easily besetting and hindering you. Legion usually meant hundreds or thousands. In the bible the devils were released from the man into a herd of about 2000 swine that ran over the cliff to their death. However, that was the number of swine, this still does not depict how many demons entered each swine, was it 1 or 10 for each pig. So see the point is if Jesus can handle the thousands of demons or sins of 1 man, he can handle whatever mine and yours are. Come to him and be delivered today. It is possible for him to deliver and restore each of us not by our works, but according to his love, grace and mercy as he did this man in the bible, who had not done one work for the Lord at this time. Shout Hallelujah and Amen.

With God all things are possible. Our sufficiency, our completeness is in him alone and his finished works for us and in us when we believe in Jesus Christ as our Lord and Saviour. You see you just canceled that blessing of God opening up the windows of heaven and pouring out a blessing that there shall not be room enough to receive it, because although you tithed, you broke the other law of thou shalt not gossip, backbite, have impure thoughts like lust, etc. whichever the other law is that you lack or fall short in, if you trying to live by the letter of the law.

Remember you break one, you have broken them all. If you live by the law, and think you are justified before God by the law, you must keep them all, and if you do not, then you are cursed under the law.

You get nothing from God if you are living under the curse of the Law. For under the curse of the Law you must do all things, every one of them, do not break not one.

****But, Thanks be to God for fulfillment by faith in Christ, by Grace.

Above he said, we are guilty of breaking all laws even if we fall short in only one. This is why he said, so live a life that you know that you are judged by the law of liberty-which is by Christ and Grace-Faith, not on how well you have maintained good works.

So that when we do 10 good deeds but have failed in keeping the other 5,000 plus. God can still look at our Faith and say here is your blessing, according to his grace and mercy and our faith in Christ Jesus. Whereas, if he was looking at the deeds/the works, each individually, in a day, to decide whether or not to bless us, we still would not get a thing from him. Why? Because he would discover that we have broken one or more intentionally or unintentionally of his laws.

There is a struggle with trying to live under the law instead of under Grace. God designed it to be so. He called us to a place of rest by Christ and in Christ, not to a place of struggle. This is why he said, Enter into thy rest and Come and I will give you rest.

You place yourselves under a curse and bondage when you try to adhere to laws by the letter that Christ has fulfilled. This may be why you hear a preacher say, wow the room went cold when they started preaching on tithes and offering by the letter or on being cursed if they do not pay them. It is because the bondage and cursing of the law has entered the room, trying to place the believer that is under Grace back under the bondage and curse of accomplishing the law by the letter when this law has been fulfilled by Christ. He whom the Son sets free is free indeed.

Many may say, this is teaching for those who just don't want to obey God and pay 10% or more of their income. They just don't want to be obedient. They just don't know what generous means.

No, this is wrong. God is saying this is teaching for those who want to obey God and fulfill the law of tithe and offering 100% by faith and no longer live under the bondages and curses of the law that was only to be our school master until Jesus came. This is teaching for those who want to live in the liberty that Christ came to provide for us while still giving as he stirs their heart to give generously according to his definition and no longer man's.

Read:Galatians 5:1-4

Let's look at the following scripture too that Christ used to show us how much better it is for us to choose to live under GRACE and not the Law, and to see how Jesus was trying to show them,just how difficult is is for them to continue to try to live under the law instead of under his Grace. Christ knew the heart of every man. He told them in times past it was told do not commit adultery, now he says, you don't have to commit the act, if you even look at her with lust, it's just like you committed the act. He knew how many had looked on in lust of things. Just looking, they, even doing that, had sinned, and now too were required to cut and pluck out eyes and cut off hands for just looking. Christ just messed them all up. I do believe he had proved his point. Choose to live under Grace and not Law.

Matthew 5:27 Ye have heard that It was said by them of old time, thou shalt not commit adultery. But I say unto you, that whosoever looketh on a woman to lust after her hath committed adultery with her already in his heart. And if thy right eye offend thee, pluck it out, and cast *it* from thee: for it is profitable for thee that one of thy members should perish, and not *that* thy whole body should be cast into hell. And if thy right hand offend thee, cut it off, and cast *it* from thee: for it is profitable for thee that one of thy members should perish, and not *that* thy whole body should be cast into hell.

Now why isn't there more eyes plucked out and hands cut off. Oh, I know why. You now believe you live under Grace and not the law, because there is no way you are plucking out your eye and cutting off your hand. No, No. Now you say Hallelujah thank you Jesus for the Grace and fulfillment of the Law.

Well the same thing with Tithe and Offering. It was the law. It was a divine carnal ordinance of the Old Covenant and Old Tabernacle that was at that time to be done by the letter, just like the sprinkling of blood around the door posts were to be done. How many of you still sprinkle blood around the doorposts to celebrate Passover. Don't go there. Shhhh. Don't tell that story. You don't, and I don't either. We understand we now, live under Grace and under a New Covenant and a New Tabernacle. We do not have to sprinkle blood around the door post. The blood of Jesus has been sprinkled over our lives. Christ fulfilled that carnal ordinance by the Spirit. He also fulfilled the grain and burnt offering as well as the tithe and offering.

God did not want them to pluck out their eyes and cut off their hands, he was trying to show them how difficult it would be for them to live under the Law when he, Grace had come, when fulfillment of the Law by Christ had come.

The law was designed to spotlight our sins, and make us aware of the things that are sin before our holy God, and then to show us how weak and inept we are in keeping these laws and not sinning, with and without him. However, we need to choose the struggle against sin with him rather than the struggle against sin without him. We have power, help, mercy and grace with him. We have none of this without him. The struggle with sin is real, as Paul proclaimed, but Christ is with us, and his compassions and mercies are new every day

Read Romans Chapters 7 thru 8 and you will see Paul describing the war that he was constantly in trying to do the good, that is in him to do, by the power of the Spirit, but he keeps succumbing to the wrong sinful flesh ways, instead of yielding to the Spirit. Paul was glad that his blessings were not tied to how well he performed but tied to whom he had believed in only. Paul said while in this body, we are constantly in the struggle of the war of Flesh warring against the Spirit. Paul admitted sometimes the flesh wins. Paul admits sometimes the thing he should do, though the spirit is in him to help him do it, he admits sometimes he still fall short and yields to his flesh. He found it a real struggle. Then he praised God, for being so good to him and to us, by

sending Christ to be our right standing for us always inspite of ourselves. Understand when we sin, God loves us so much he will still chastise us to get us back into his will. This is still his blessing us through his love and patience, mercy and compassions, for he could just in an instant consume us. This helps us grow and mature in Christ and become more adept to doing things in the Spirit and less to the flesh. It helps us grow up in God from the milk infancy stage to being able to digest meat and to grow from the weak faith Christian to the Strong faith Christian. Thanks be to God for his longsuffering, his patience, mercy and compassion every day.

<u>Read Lamentations 3:22</u>

THINGS I'VE LEARNED

CHAPTER 4

●

IN THE HEART BY THE SPIRIT 'VS' NOT BY THE
LETTER, A STRONGER FAITH VS A WEAKER FAITH.
NEITHER IS SIN-BOTH ARE UNTO THE LORD. NEITHER
IS A FALSE GOD, OR A FALSE PROPHET OR A FALSE
TEACHER. IT IS MAN'S CONDEMNATION NOT GOD'S
CONDEMNATION

<u>Read the following:</u>

<u>Read 2 Corinthians 3:1-10</u> Do we begin again to commend
ourselves? or need we, as some *others*, epistles of commendation
to you, or *letters* of commendation from you? Ye are our epistle
written in our hearts, known and read of all men *Forasmuch as ye
are* manifestly declared to be the epistle of Christ ministered by us,
written not with ink, but with the Spirit of the living God; not in
tables of stone, but in fleshy tables of the heart And such trust have
we through Christ to God– Not that we are sufficient of ourselves
to think anything as of ourselves; but our sufficiency *is* of God; Who
also hath **made us able ministers of the new testament; not
of the letter, but of the spirit: for the letter killeth, but the
spirit giveth life. But if the ministration of death, written
and engraven in stones, was glorious, so that the children
of Israel could not stedfastly behold the face of Moses for
the glory of his countenance; which *glory* was to be done
away: How shall not the ministration of the spirit be rather
glorious? For if the ministration of condemnation *be* glory,
much more doth the ministration of righteousness exceed**

in glory. For even that which was made glorious had no glory in this respect, by reason of the glory that excelleth.

Read Roman 7:4-6 also

What does in the heart / in the Spirit and not of the letter mean in the above verses?

Not of the letter but of the Spirit of Christ, the Holy Spirit, means, the Israelites no longer had to continue to keep the old carnal ordinances and regulations of the Old Tabernacle under the Old Covenant. They could continue to operate under the old system. It would not be a sin but it would be bondage to them. It would not be wrong, but very difficult for them. They had to receive Christ, or they would still be condemned to hell, even if they kept the Mosaic law by the letter..

Even, after they received Christ, they no longer had to observe the old Festivals of Sabbath, Passover and many other festivals we will discuss later, and they did not have to continue to bring animal sacrifices, and the tithe and offerings that were carnal ordinances under the law for the old tabernacle. The Old Tabernacle Laws of being circumcised in the flesh, of bringing tithe and offerings of the land and animals, of paying redemption money, atonement money, tithe and offering and many laws as such, they no longer had to do those things by the letter. They no longer had to refrain from eating certain meats. They did not have to continue to observe certain days. They no longer had to keep from touching or handling things that would defile them, and so forth. Why? Because, all these things had now been completed by the indwelling of the Holy Spirit by Christ. We see Jesus, showing this concept on the Sabbath, where he himself did not keep the Sabbath, by the letter, for he knew he had fulfilled that in himself.

These were some of the Old Tabernacle laws and Old Festival laws that were no longer required to be done outwardly,

i.e. By the letter. These specific laws all had been fulfilled inwardly by the indwelling of the Holy Spirit.

However, they were told they still had to perform the moral laws of the land/government, by the letter.

The laws of the land and government were the laws like thou shalt not kill, steal, commit adultery, etc. These type of laws were still required to be done outwardly, by the letter.

See the issue has been when we say we no longer have to do some of the Tabernacle and Festival laws, we group automatically all the Land/Government Laws with this statement, and this has been error.

We still must keep by the letter the Land/Government Laws by the letter although they also are fulfilled by the Spirit. Some of the old laws of biblical times also are not required in our new laws of the land today either. You do not see the plucking out of eyes and cutting off of hands that were in the biblical days being done today. Glory to God for his grace.

So, we see the following points.

1. All laws completed/fulfilled/not abolished/not ended/ but better FULFILLED by Christ by Grace. Laws of the Tabernacle and Laws of the Festivals, and Laws of the Land/ Government by the Spirit of God through Christ Jesus. **(Read Mark 12:28-34)-**All the law completed by our loving God and one another. The only way I can love God or another is that I receive Jesus Christ as my Lord and Saviour, receive his Holy Spirit in my heart, then I have the Love of God and the Love for God, given by God for us, for him and for another. Glory to God.

2. We see that the Old Tabernacle Laws and Festivals, no longer have to be done by the Letter, **but if you choose to**

continue them, it is not a sin if you do and it is not a sin if you don't. All must believe on Jesus Christ.

There are no churches I know that pay redemption and atonement money, or bring the blood of goats and bulls or offer burnt offerings, or grain offerings. There are not many churches that still sprinkle blood around their doors in observance of Passover. There are not many that adhere to all the old requirements of the Sabbath in the biblical days. Why is this? Because they understand what Grace has done for the World, in fulfillment, and that those thing are no longer required by the letter.. It is the same thing with Tithe and Offering. Tithe and offering was a law under the Old Tabernacle Laws. However, Giving, is still required under the New Tabernacle and New Covenant. It is not a set percentage. It is a free giving as one purposes in their heart, as their hearts are stirred by God to freely and cheerfully give, and to be set aside at the beginning of each week according as God has prospered each of us. Do not use this scripture point of, as God has prospered each of us, to get into other people financial business. This simply means it all has come from the hand of God. It is simply recognizing God as the source from which our prosperity comes. God will still stir each heart to give according to God's guidance on each individual. We are all to be led by the direction of God and not by the condemnation, judgement, persecution, criticism, opinions and reproach of man.

3. We see that if any of the Laws of the Land/Government which were separate from the Laws/Ordinances of the Tabernacle and Festival laws, were broken it could mean death, or they would then have to take a specific offering to the Tabernacle according to the Laws of the Tabernacle, in order to be cleansed and forgiven of that sin from the law they had broken. Laws such as you must not steal, kill, commit adultery, etc. and so forth were laws of the land. Although laws such as previously stated are still in effect today and must and should be adhered to, we also know

that many of their laws of the land and government in biblical days, do not apply to us today. As time has evolved, new laws in current society have been adapted for the betterment of our society but there are also laws today that have been passed that are against the will of God. We must always choose to obey God and not man, as we submit to the governing authorities and laws today. This is what the Hebrew boys chose to do, as they choose not to follow the law of the government to worship other idols, they chose to instead follow God and not submit to the King's idols, although he was the governing authority of the land. They chose not to bow down to him as their god/idol. They were thrown in the fiery furnace for holding to their conviction, but God spared their life. Another disciple Stephen was killed for holding to his convictions. We must choose to always obey God in all things. No matter what the situation is, no matter what may or may not happen to or for us. We must choose to always obey God well in all things, even if it means, losing the house, the fame and fortune,friends, and family, or even if it means gaining enemies, or even if it means death for us as Stephen and Christ chose to do. **(Read Titus 2:7-15)**

The people, and the Pharisees, and Sadducees, could not receive this and begin to plot ways as to how they might kill Paul because of this teaching. They also killed Jesus for him teaching the same thing about who he was and what he had come to do. Not abolish the Law but fulfill the Law.

Read:
Matthew 5:17 Think not that I am come to destroy the law, or the prophets: I am not come to destroy, but to fulfill.
They could not grasp what God had done for the world by Grace sending Jesus our Lord and Saviour to all who would believe in him to fulfill all these things in us.

Read the following scriptures to understand what the Spirit of Christ dwelling in us has set us free from doing by the letter.

Read also Colossians 2:16- 22

We are saying I have been saved, I believe in Christ, but I am not going to stop tithing by the letter, I am not going to stop preparing the burnt offerings for the Sabbath, I am not going to start eating this and that meat, I am not going to stop sprinkling blood around the doorposts for Passover, I still can't touch this animal or that because I will be defiled by it, or because if I do, God will curse me. God will punish me.

This is not true, as we have already discussed. We are still thinking in the carnal mind on spirit matters. We are still living by the letter of the law of the old tabernacle rules. God says walk in the renewed mind. He says walk in the mind of the Spirit not the mind of the carnal. Walk in your grace and not in the law. We are thinking we have to carry things out by the letter when God said he has fulfilled them by his Spirit in us. This is what is meant in the above scripture not of the letter, but of the Spirit, for the letter killeth, but the spirit giveth life.

This does not mean we are not to walk in love by the letter, we still are to walk in love always, even though all law is fulfilled by the Spirit.

We are not understanding what Christ has become to us and for us through our faith in him, and his Holy Spirit and his Grace towards us, or should I say we understand for some areas, just not for other areas.

We today are the saved Pharisees with this thinking. We live the lives of the saved Pharisees.

They believed on Christ but told Peter that Gentiles must still keep the law of Moses and be circumcised. This is what is still being taught in our churches today. Peter said no this is not true. Peter addresses them in the following scriptures.

Read:

Acts 15:5 But there rose up certain of the sect of the Pharisees which believed, saying, That it was needful to circumcise them, and to command them to keep the law of Moses.

Some of the Pharisees who had believed in Jesus, were now saying that the Gentiles had to not only believe in Christ but keep the Mosaic law, and all the old regulations and carnal ordinances of the Old Tabernacle.

We see in the next scripture Peter rises against the believing Pharisees and tell them that they are doing wrong by trying to persuade the Gentiles to follow the law of Moses and its ordinances after they have believed on Jesus and received the Holy Ghost from God. Peter said the Pharisees were trying to put a yoke on the Gentiles that neither the Pharisees, or their fathers had been able to bear by the letter.

Read the rest of this chapter for more understanding.

After believing in Christ and being saved. You and I are not to revert back to trying to keep the law and ordinances in order to stay in right standing. We are to continue to maintain good works of the law and continue to walk in brotherly love according to the law, but the carnal ordinances no longer had to be kept by the letter. Christ fulfilled it all for us. Christ and his blood keeps us in right standing. He was the end of the law for righteousness. He places and keeps us perfect before the eyes of our holy God. He became our Sabbath, which is why he said come to me and find Rest. The Sabbath represented days of rest from their works. Christ is our Rest. He wants us to enter into this rest and remain in his rest. Stop turning back to the law that is removing us from our rest. Stay in your rest. Stay in your Grace. All he requires, if we fall short and sin, which he does not desire for us to do, but if we do, he requires us to come to his throne of grace and find mercy, confess our sin, turn from our sin and he is faithful and just to forgive and cleanse us from all our sins and transgressions, presenting us faultless before the Father forever, as he is our advocate.

Paul addressed this concern in Galatians. He asked them why do you think after being saved, placed in right standing by faith and grace by Christ, that it then becomes your responsibility to stay in right standing, to stay perfect before God, by keeping the ordinances of bringing the tithes and offering, observing the Sabbaths, etc. by the letter, because this is not true. I have satisfied these things. Accept what the sacrifice of Christ has brought us into.

Many also have been scared also thinking that if they are saved and do not do these things they will not enter into heaven, even after believing in The Lord Christ, because the word says all that say Lord, Lord shall not enter into heaven. All that cast out devils in his name shall not enter into heaven. I use to be scared to death. I thought this meant there is still a chance, after I have believed in Christ, I can get to heaven, and still be cast into the burning Hell. So now I was faced with how well can I keep these ordinances without breaking any so I can make it in. I was failing miserably at this. I kept missing it, either this law or that. I was sweating bullets, so were you, and some of you still are. I was never sure of my salvation, because I was back to trying to perform the Works of the Law to get in rather than be assured of my status that was by faith in Christ alone. None of us should be saved and scared like this. This should not be.
I have learned better. I am no longer in fear. I am sure of my salvation. I strive everyday to maintain good works, but I still miss it at times, but I know now also, I can confess, repent and go boldly to my Father for grace, mercy and forgiveness, because Jesus is my advocate, daily, if I do fall short and sin. Everyone can live in this peace and Grace. God does not want us to intentionally enter into sin. Never are we to think that. However, he does want us to

understand what our relationship is with him under Grace when we do miss it.

Notice I said when we miss it, not if we miss it. We all miss it at times.

Romans 3:23 For all have sinned, and come short of the glory of God;

Let's look at this scripture.

Matthew 7:21-23 Not every one that saith unto me, Lord, Lord, shall enter into the kingdom of heaven; but he that doeth the will of my Father which is in heaven. Many will say to me in that day, Lord, Lord, have we not prophesied in thy name? and in thy name have cast out devils? and in thy name done many wonderful works? And then will I profess unto them, I never knew you: depart from me, ye that work iniquity.

If we read these verses alone. It seems like he is talking to the saved man, by the terminology, it is someone calling the Master Lord, Lord, and they say they have been prophesying and casting out devils in his name. Only believers do that right? No. False prophets do as well. Let's look at the full picture,
I encourage you to read the full chapter of Matthew 24. It tells us how we cannot be deceived by the false prophets who will come as Christ said, and they will say their name is JESUS CHRIST, and they will do many wonders and signs with their magic, witchcraft etc, but they are frauds. They are wolves in sheep clothing.

When he, Christ comes, he will not make an announcement as he said.

So after reading the full context. We understand that there is a case of Identity theft going on.

The false prophets have stolen the identity of Jesus Christ. They are going across the countries telling everyone their name is Jesus Christ and they are THE CHRIST, the Messiah. They are going to be so deceived in themselves in the end they are actually going to try to say to the Master himself. But Lord, Lord, did we not cast out demons in your name and prophesy in your name, knowing they never believed in the Savior for themselves, knowing they were wicked and had stolen his identity. They just had stolen his identity, and was walking down on the earth claiming to be Him, saying ye, I am the Christ. I am the one. They were full of sorcery, magic, and witch craft and had been able to perform some signs and wonders before the people. By this evil magic and sorcery they deceived many. They never confessed him as Lord and Saviour, they never believed in him. They just stole his identity and was doing magic deceiving the people

It is the false prophets that he will say depart from me I never knew you. Not those who confessed the Lord Jesus and believed on him in their heart. He was referring to the false prophets only.

Remember, Blessed Assurance. If you have believed in Jesus, the Son of God, as your Lord and Saviour, you are going to spend eternity in Heaven with the Father, as he promised to all who would believe in Jesus.

Read:

Exodus 7:10 -12 And Moses and Aaron went in unto Pharaoh, and they did so as the LORD had commanded: and Aaron cast down his rod before Pharaoh, and before his servants, and it became a serpent, Then Pharaoh also called the wise men and the sorcerers: now the magicians of Egypt, they also did in like manner with their enchantments. For they cast down every man his rod, and they became serpents: but Aaron's rod swallowed up their rods

See there will be false prophets like the false prophets in Moses and Aaron times. They had magic and sorcery, and the same things that

Moses and Aaron did, they did. However, God had the serpents of Aaron and Moses overcome the False Prophets serpents. God cannot be defeated, or deceived and neither can his true children of faith.

This is what is meant in the end days, yes, there will be False Prophets coming in the name of Christ, doing magic, etc. But they are not the real Messiah. Do not be deceived.

Another scripture that is being used against God's people if they do not keep the Sabbath, and tithe and offering, and many of the other festivals and other ordinances of old and even if you, as a believer, miss the mark and sin, intentionally or unintentionally, the following scripture is being used to strip the believer of our salvation and cast us into the pit of hell forever. This was the one used on me. Made me think I was destined for Hell for sure, even after having believed in Christ, been baptized, and was trying to live right, but yes I felt the struggle between the flesh and the spirit and I did miss it at times, and when I missed it I heard the sister's and brother's quoting this scripture.

1 Corinthians 6:9-12 Know ye not that the **unrighteous shall not inherit the kingdom of God?** Be not deceived: neither fornicators, nor idolaters, nor adulterers, nor effeminate, nor abusers of themselves with mankind, Nor thieves, nor covetous, nor drunkards, nor revilers, nor extortioners, shall inherit the kingdom of God. **And such were some of you: but ye are washed, but ye are sanctified, but ye are justified in the name of the Lord Jesus, and by the Spirit of our God**. All things are lawful unto me, but all things are not expedient: all things are lawful for me, but I will not be brought under the power of any

This scripture too has been taught that if any is a fornicator, adultery, thief, covetous, drunkard, etc. after being saved, has fallen from grace and is back to their unrighteous state and will go to hell and shall not see the kingdom of God. This is incorrect.

I was scared to death. The fire was vivid. I was a babe in Christ. I didn't know how secure my standing was and they did not help me either quoting this scripture to me.

Thanks be to God through prayer and studying to show myself a workman not ashamed, but rightly dividing the word of truth, by the grace of God who gave me understanding. I know I am heaven bound forever. I know I got an advocate with the Father, in Jesus. If I miss it, I don't have to stay in the pit, I can arise and get boldly before the throne of heaven, repent, confess, get forgiven, and get back in the game for my Jesus.

Yes, in (1 Corinthians 6:9-12) - this scripture is talking to the righteous. He is using this as a comparison to how the believers in Corinth were acting at the time, as if they were the unrighteous and not the righteousness of God. They were not acting like the people of God but like the heathen unbeliever.They were continuing in their sin without sorrow or repentance and this was not pleasing. He reminded the righteous of their status. He reminded the righteous they were not the same creature any longer since Christ had come into their lives. They should be living as such. He reminded them they are not like the unrighteous who will not inherit the kingdom, since they are now the righteousness of God. So he wanted to know why were they acting like the unrighteous. He told the believers in Corinth, yes you were like this at one time. We all were. You and I included. Until Christ came and justified us. Now although there is nothing that can separate us from his love. This does not mean I should do every thing as if I was an unbeliever n my old nature before Christ came into my life. I am a new creation. The people in Corinth were doing all these awful things that the unrighteous do. Here were the righteous doing what they used to do when they were not saved. Paul was telling them they should not be doing such things. He was reprimanding them, rebuking them, chastising them, correcting them so they would come to repentance. He was not telling them they had lost their salvation because they had sinned.

He was not telling them they were saved but going to still go to Hell. He was telling them to stop sinning and walk as the ambassadors of Christ they are. We are to live as examples, and light of holiness and righteousness for Christ before all believers and unbelievers.

2 Corinthians 5:20 Now then we are ambassadors for Christ, as though God did beseech *you* by us: we pray *you* in Christ's stead, be ye reconciled to God.

Hebrews 12:14 Follow peace with all *men*, and holiness, without which no man shall see the Lord:

Stronger faith vs Weaker Faith

Another way the devil has the believers in strife against one another is because one is stronger in their faith in areas of grace and one is weaker in their faith in areas of grace, and both begin to condemn the other and begin to label the other as a false teacher, a false prophet, teaching false doctrine or accuse one another as following a false God. Both, the weaker faith Christian and the strong faith Christian are pleasing and acceptable unto God in the works that they do. Neither is sinning, if one continues the tithing ordinance by the Letter or not. One is simply stronger in their understanding of the scriptures and another is not. Neither the weaker or the stronger are to condemn the other. They are to find the things they do agree on and walk accordingly and leave the rest up to God to make his servants understand and grow their faith stronger as we continue to pray for one another. **This is what God commanded us in Romans chapter 14 and 1 Corinthians chapter 8**.

That which is fulfilled in the heart by the Spirit is more powerful and glorious than that which was done by the letter. The stronger in faith understands the fulfillment of the Tithe and offering, through the grace and faith of Christ.

The stronger is to give the weaker in faith understanding of this fulfillment but not condemn their weaker brethren. Neither is the weaker to condemn the stronger in their understanding of this principle of fulfillment of Tithe and offering by Grace.

This is exactly what the enemy has done in the body of Christ today. He has pitted the Stronger and weaker Christian against one another and said choose because one is sinning. However, God says, when both are believers, neither is sinning in this area of Tithing, one is only weaker and the other stronger. Tithing 10% by the letter is not a sin, just as understanding that you no longer are bound to the law of giving 10% by the letter because as a believer this has been fulfilled 100% by Christ in you. You can still give 10% but you won't be cursed if you don't .

Now, I know how some of you think, so lets correct that faulty thinking now. This is different when we are talking about a topic that is actual sin.

If you are both believers and either or both is stealing, killing, and committing adultery, or any other sexual sin or you know your sin, name it, etc. and either tries to correct the other, this is not a case of weaker and stronger, this is a case of someone is actually sinning and bringing correction to one another. This is doctrine, we in the church should be told by the other that it is sin and that we need to turn from it, pray for one another, walk in love with each other, and not mock the correction of God by calling one another hypocrites, and watch God do what only he can do in one another lives as we obey the word of the Lord spoken to us by another believer.

So, do not call something that is clearly sin and say oh I am not sinning, I am just a weak Christian in this area. Yes, you are weak in this area, but the thing you are doing of stealing, and lying is still a sin that you need to correct.

Now, not every area we are weak in is a sin. I may be weak in my faith in flying on an airplane, or riding on a horse or riding in a car with a race car driver, or jumping out of airplanes, or climbing mountains, or camping in the woods. Just because my faith is weak in these areas and yours is not, does not mean you are sinning because you do them all, and neither does it mean I am sinning because I don't do them. Do you get the picture. God will not be mocked. He will deal with each of us for those things which are sins.

THINGS I'VE LEARNED

CHAPTER 5

NO LICENSE TO SIN

We have been saved to live lives in holiness and righteousness as ambassadors for God

Read the following:
Galatians 5:13-14 For brethren you have been called unto liberty only use not liberty for an occasion to flesh.

1 Peter 1:16 Because it is written, Be ye holy; for I am holy.

Luke 1: 74-75 That he would grant unto us, that we being delivered out of the hand of our enemies might serve him without fear, In holiness and righteousness before him, all the days of our life.

He shows us in his word, though he is the fulfillment, we are still to love and walk out that love towards our neighbor by doing good works. We must still not have the faith of our Lord in vain. Walk according to the Spirit that is dwelling in us, not walking according to our flesh.

James 2:1 My brethren, have not the faith of our Lord Jesus Christ, *the Lord* of glory, with respect of persons.

James 2:17 Even so faith, if hath not works, is dead, being alone.

We do have to maintain good works and walk in love, by the enablement of the Holy Spirit. However, we must understand our blessings are still not based on us doing works. It is only based on us having Christ in our hearts, and his grace and his mercy. Just like we were not saved based on our works, we still are not receiving our blessings and the fulfillment of his promises because we maintain good works. We receive all the blessings only by grace of God by the blood of Jesus –in whom this grace came because of our Faith in him, and this faith also was a gift from God.

See even in the above scripture, God is showing us that in the New Covenant, yes, we still must maintain good works and walk in love, yes we must have faith with works. However, His blessings are never based on our works. Our works show we have placed our Faith in Christ. It is only based on our Faith in Christ which is why we do the works.

We need to be thankful always for this. For we are still flesh and we still fall short daily in our struggle between the Flesh and Spirit. You see, maintaining good works is our reasonable service to the Lord. He called us. He chose us to display his power and glory, his character on, in and through us in his ways. Sometimes we don't understand his ways, but he says Trust him and lean not to our own understanding. He is the Potter and we are the clay in his hands. He can use us as he chooses in his plans for his purposes. He tells us don't grow weary in well doing. He tells us to Trust God FOREVER. No matter what happens in this life to us and our loved ones, never turn from following God. He is always using our lives to display his power, forgiveness, patience, long suffering, compassion, love, kindness, giving heart etc. to the world, reconciling the world back to himself through us and our lives, that as they see us adorn the doctrine of Christ in every situation that happens to us, every situation that God allows to touch our lives, the Good and the Bad, they see Christ in us and want him as their Lord and Saviour as well. Don't ever stop doing the right things for his sake. Jesus didn't stop, and he suffered the cross for us all. He is our greatest example to follow.

To help us in our struggle against sin we must understand that although we are in the world, we do not have a license to sin like the world. We are in the world but not of this world. We are in the flesh but we are also in the Spirit. We have to remember God is always looking at the Spirit of Christ dwelling in us that is perfect in every way, and wants us to look at ourselves as he sees us in the Spirit not in the Flesh. This is called walking in the newness of our spirit and walking in the spirit mind not the carnal mind.

Romans 8:5 -6 For they that are after the flesh do mind the things of the flesh; but they that are after the Spirit the things of the Spirit For to be carnally minded *is* death; but to be spiritually minded *is* life and peace.

We must walk in the newness of our spirit and mind.

However, every day we tend to look at ourselves in the Flesh and Carnal more than in the Spirit man. We must renew our mind in this area and grow from the milk stage in leaning more to the carnal and mature to the meat stage of leaning more to doing things according to the Spirit of God.

The 1ˢᵗ Picture-For a believer to see is this picture .This is –How God Sees me Daily.When God looks at me daily, this is What and Who God sees. This is who I actually am in his eyes-As a believer. He sees Christ ALONE. He sees fulfillment of all the Law. He sees perfection. He sees No sin. Why, because I am hid in Christ. He don't see ME.

This is the only picture God sees of you and I when we are a believer.

So now when we fall short. Confess, ask God for forgiveness, repent, turn back, don't condemn, don't hang your head for 2 weeks. Let the blood cleanse you. Get back to maintaining the good works that you have to still do. Repeat, Repeat, Repeat. If necessary and trust it will be necessary till you get to heaven. Remember God's grace does not always mean we will not have to deal with some consequences or chastisement for our disobedience. Amen.

2nd picture- What I –in the flesh actually do daily as a believer, as a struggle in this sinful world.

I live in the body and mind which is the carrnal/flesh, with the Spirit. I work to maintain good works. I do not want to sin. I do not want to make a mistake. I want to please my Saviour in every way, but sometimes I fall short. Will this ever end while I am the flesh? No, it will not. I have the power to not sin through the Holy Spirit. Which is why God tells us to go and sin no more, because as believers, if we yield to the Holy Spirit in us telling us, no don't do that, each time we will be able to keep ourselves from sin. However, we still are in the carnal/flesh body while at the same time living in the Spirit, and the struggle is real. We don't always yield to that small still voice, the Holy Spirit. We instead fall to that Yell from our flesh. We all have missed the mark and will miss it many times before we get to heaven. This is why I have to strive to continue to do good, but if I do miss the mark, I have to remember the 1st picture of who I truly am in Christ, who is my advocate, as a believer. I am hid in Christ. The Father sees the Son. So now when I fall short, unintentionally or intentionally. I need to repent, turn back, Confess, ask God for forgiveness.

The wrath of God will come upon children of disobedience. God will not be mocked. Is there mercy with God. Yes, there is. However, do not test and tempt the Lord thy God at any time.

Read: Colossians 3:6 For which things' sake the wrath of God cometh on the children of disobedience

In the carnal/flesh—as Paul said, I/We still find ourselves doing good in a lot of area. I mean we are being successful in a lot of areas, but at the same time we are falling short in a lot of areas as well, whether it is a wrong thought that we have to cast down, whether it is looking at another with lust in our heart, whether it is being jealous, and covetous, bitterness, guilt, shame, doubt, whatever it is. Paul said when I would do right, I seem to find myself doing wrong. O wretched man am I.

This is why we must remember the 1ˢᵗ Picture-of How God sees us and encourage one another in the Lord and encourage ourselves in the Lord and repent and get back on track for we are still in right standing with the Lord.

However, that is not what is happening. Let's be honest, Instead we are saying things like you didn't pay your tithes well God has not changed, you are robbing him and he has cursed you. You will not see any blessings from his great treasures of heaven until you turn back to him as he said. This is not true.
We are Forgetting this Law of tithing is no longer to be done <u>by the letter</u> it is fulfilled in us <u>by the Spirit dwelling in us.</u>

Once a believer in Christ. You do not lose your righteousness before God. What can separate me from the love of God. NOTHING.

<u>Romans 8:31-39</u>

We sin, yes we do. We are not to have fellowship with unrighteousness, when we have the Spirit of God in us, No we are not. But we do not lose fellowship with God or our salvation. How is that? It is because of Christ. That if a man sins as a believer, look at what happens.

<u>1 John 2:1</u> My little children, these things write I unto you, that ye sin not. And if any man sin, we have an advocate with the Father, Jesus Christ the righteous: And he is the propitiation for our sins: and not for ours only, but also for *the sins of* the whole world

This is why many don't turn back, because they think by them walking away from God, they ended their fellowship and salvation with God, and there is no hope for them now, but no, you as a believer by sinning cannot end your fellowship with God,unless you by some power can remove the Holy Spirit that was given as a deposit forever into your life to seal your fellowship and salvation. God never moved just because you moved, and your moving still did not remove the Holy Spirit from your life. Therefore, you did not remove your name from the Book of Life.

He identifies us as his forever by the seal of the Holy Spirit in our hearts. We have lied to ourselves and said I am no longer in fellowship with God, We have said to ourselves I have lost my salvation, because of our wrongly dividing of the word. We have to stop saying these curses over our lives and stop allowing the enemy to prevail over us when God has given us his daily victory in Christ. You have sinned. In other words you have been disobedient to his words, but disobedience is not the end of fellowship or salvation. It is simply disobedience that must be corrected with confession and repentance, and see the love, grace and mercy of God pardon, strengthen, and help you move forward. Why, because he promised to never leave nor forsake us.

Read:
2 Corinthians 1:22 Who hath also sealed us, and given the earnest of the Spirit in our hearts.

Remember too he has promised he will always be with us, as believers even unto the end of the earth.

Matthew 28:20 Teaching them to observe all things whatsoever I have commanded you: and, lo, I am with you alway, *even* unto the end of the world. Amen.

It is because of this continuous fellowship via the Holy Spirit that God comes after us in his love for us telling us to turn from sin. We too are disobedient children that our God has to correct at times, but he never disconnects from us.

Our God loves us so much, if we refuse to correct our ways and turn back to him when we are believers, he knows how to makes us stand. He loves us so much, he will chastise us till we turn from our sins. If someone does not stop the sin as a believer and dies, he still will see Jesus face to face and not for condemnation to hell, but because he chose Christ while he or she was living as their Lord and Saviour they will still go to heaven for eternity. He does this because of the fellowship we still share as his children with him our Father. He does this because of the salvation that he gave us sealing us by his Spirit for eternity as his children forever. We are his sons and daughters. He is with us always. Never leaves us. Never forsakes us. He will never cast us out. He will always have arms wide opened as the prodigal son's father had for him. We can't leave him, we can't walk away from him either, for his Spirit is in us everywhere, no matter how disobedient we become. Remember disobedience to God never works out in our favor. His chastisement is greater sometimes then we want.

You say what about my cousin that was saved but walked away from the Lord and got strung out on drugs. He lost his fellowship. No, God was in hot pursuit to turn them around. What if they die in this state of drug addiction, and they were saved. Will they go to heaven? Did the thief on the cross with Jesus, go to heaven. Yes, and the thief was saved that moment when he believed on Jesus on the Cross, and Jesus said this day will I see you in Paradise. Why? Because he promised the same wage of Eternal Life to every one that believed on him, whether they started working at 8:00 am or not until 4:25 with quitting time 4:30. Remember the parable about the man who hired men to work for him and paid them equally no matter the time they received his offer to work for him. **Matthew 20.** People complained then and they still complaining about the perfect will of God._That drug addicted cousin that was saved but died in their addiction. They will be with the Father when they die, just as God promised them because of their faith in Jesus. If grandma was healed when she got to heaven, trust me that cousin is not a drug addict in heaven. God is faithful.

We then have to accept that God used them in a different way, even through the drug addiction. Maybe it was to show the world how the enemy can rob the life, and cause all kinds of havoc on earth for a believer that is not obedient to the Lord, which none should want to endure since Christ came to give us so much better in this life on earth as well as eternal life. Maybe he wanted to show the enemy still cannot rob this same believer of their salvation. The enemy may be able to rob us of many things, but not our salvation. This is why God shows us the great man Job in the bible who lost many things, became angry with God but he clung to his God through his faith through it all.

God's plan is not drug addiction for anyone, but the devil's plan is. God always speaks to us to not to sin, but many fail to heed to the voice, fail to obey the voice of the Holy Spirit and get caught in Satan's trap. Glory to God for his faithfulness. He may chastise us for our wrong decisions in life as any good father should and will do. However, he will always forgive us, and show us his grace and mercy. God has promised to give us beauty for our ashes. He is our redeemer after every mistake in life. After every sin, if we will just turn back to him and repent and confess our sins. His arms are always opened.

God is Sovereign. He is the Potter and we are the clay. Ask Job, Ask Stephen, Ask John the Baptist. We come to understand his ways and that he will use some one way and others in another. This is why he tells us to trust him and lean not to our own understanding, but understand he said in all things he is glorified, through all that we experience and endure while in this world, good and bad . Walk by this Faith, this word he has spoken and not by sight. All glory to God for our never losing Fellowship with our Father as a believer.

We may walk away in the natural/carnal/flesh, but we have not walked away from God in the Spirit. This is why it is so important for us to walk/live according to the Spirit mind of thinking and no longer in the carnal minded thinking. This is why God tells us to walk in the newness of the spirit and be renewed in our mind.

David said, where can I go and you are not there. Where can I go that your spirit is not with me.

Because of Christ fulfillment, I have this forever fellowship and salvation. Never out of fellowship because of sin, because Christ made certain by his blood and Spirit that could never happen, since he became my Advocate and I became adopted as his child forever. I may be in disobedience but never out of fellowship because the Holy Spirit is always with me speaking to me and my salvation is never lost.. All you and I have to do when we become disobedient is repent, confess and be obedient.

This is what has been happening. It has been said if you don't pay tithes then you are cursed. If you don't do this, you will be punished. So now if we were still trying to use these daily works of the law to keep us in good standing, and from curses, and as a basis for our receiving blessings or cursings, we see we have broken them all EVERY DAY, and are not worthy to receive anything. However, thanks be to God for his Grace, Hallelujah, By Jesus Christ, who is our Lord and Saviour.

This is for only the believer who are in Christ Jesus. You must believe in Christ.

Now since Christ has come

*If you are not a believer. You have no other option, but condemnation, because there is no more offerings, blood sacrifices, the old way is no more. Therefore, receive Christ as Lord and Saviour today, fulfill all the law in you by the dwelling of the Holy Spirit, then continue to always strive to maintain good works daily.

*However if you are in Christ, as a believer in Christ. You are not condemned although you may fall short in your daily keeping/ maintaining of the good works.

Glory moment: Remember the 1st Picture, of how our God looks at us-we are Hid in Christ. Because Christ dwells in you. He looks not at the picture of you in the flesh and the works-alone- for right standing.

He looks at the picture of You and/ the Spirit/and sees all the Law fulfilled by the Spirit-through Christ. All the law was fulfilled by Christ in your heart. That is what Christ looks at and says you are still in right standing with me, here is the blessing and promises that are all yes and amen by Christ Jesus. Remember he will not condemn you, and he will still have mercy on you if he chooses, remember as any loving father, he may chastise us, punish us, allow us to suffer some consequences first. Chastisement is not condemnation. Remember that. There is a difference.

This is called Grace-Hallelujah

Grace and salvation has been given to us all, the Jew and Gentile, automatically when we believe in the Son of God, Jesus Christ of Nazareth. When we have faith in him. This Grace was not based on our goodness, but the goodness of our God. Grace was not based on how well we kept all the laws but based on the Grace of God by Christ Jesus alone. Grace is a true gift from our loving Father. Thanks be to God his Grace is always sufficient (enough and more than enough).Glory to his name always and forever. So sufficient that even while we were sinners he died for us.

THINGS I'VE LEARNED

CHAPTER 6

●

WALK IN LOVE

(Though Christ knew he was the Law he still walked in love with the Pharisees to not offend anyone for he had not went to heaven.) Thereby Christ was without Sin.

Matthew 17:24-27 And when they were come to Capernaum, they that received tribute *money* came to Peter, and said, Doth not your master pay tribute? He saith, Yes. And when he was come into the house, Jesus prevented him, saying, What thinkest thou, Simon? of whom do the kings of the earth take custom or tribute? of their own children, or of strangers? Peter saith unto him, Of strangers. Jesus saith unto him, Then are the children free.Notwithstanding, lest we should offend them, go thou to the sea, and cast an hook, and take up the fish that first cometh up; and when thou hast opened his mouth, thou shalt find a piece of money: that take, and give unto them for me and thee.

In maintaining good works, we all are to still Walk in Love with one another as God loved us and has commanded us to: This means continue to do good towards one another, no committing adultery, stealing, killing etc.

See many think that you teach this truth of living by the Spirit of fulfillment and not by the letter means you are telling people they have a license to sin, and live unholy lives. No, you are teaching Grace and Truth, not Sin.

Not by the letter and by the Spirit does not mean we are not to walk in love by the letter. We still are to walk in love always by the letter —meaning with an outward show.
Yes we are to maintain good works, and walk in love with one another, by the letter recognizing his fulfillment forever. Walk out the Love to one another. This Love that is indeed fulfilled by the Spirit, but is to be done by the letter daily.

Read the following scriptures on Love that follow:

Luke 10:27 And he answering said, Thou shalt love the Lord thy God with all thy heart, and with all thy soul, and with all thy strength, and with all thy mind; and thy neighbour as thyself.

Galatians 5:6 For in Christ-neither circumcision, nor uncircumcision has any value. The only thing that counts is faith expressing itself through love.

Hebrews 13:1 Let brotherly Love continue

We understand God today still has Governments and Laws set up in every country. All governments may have different laws. Laws have changed over the years as well. Read the books of Genesis through Deuteronomy of some of their laws back then. Some I am glad were ended. Some you think, thank you Lord have been kept. Some you just can't believe how terrible they were. Eye for eye, foot for foot. Oh, my goodness. Our laws under our government have changed through the years as well. Years ago women could not vote, blacks could not attend school with whites or eat in different places, etc.etc.

Thank God for his grace that those laws changed and he has given equality to all.

Now think, when the Women suffrage laws changed and when laws changed concerning the education system, did the law change of do not kill, do not steal, do not run red lights, etc. No. We knew those laws remained the same and if we broke them and the governing officers saw it or we were caught we would pay the penalities. Therefore, No, you cannot go and start killing, stealing, disobeying traffic laws, and securities exchange laws, or doing all types of sexual immoralities like whoremonging, fornicating, adultery, homoxsexuality, bisexuality, and any other form of sexual perversions, or dancing with snakes, or walking on hot coals, and you can't start breaking gravity laws thinking you can jump off top of mountains and buildings and the angels will catch you, or you can't think the angels will save you from that 18 wheeler coming right at you standing in the middle of the road, because you putting your faith and God to the test. You want to test and tempt the Lord by going 100 mph in a 60 mph zone, and all other sort of foolishness people think they can do and still say they are under Grace now and think they have a license to sin, or that they have a license to live unholy lives, or do foolishness. The devil is a lie.

Do you know what that is. It is people trying to Mock God and Tempt Him. Today's translation is this: Don't try it. Don't try the argument that we have the license to sin because we are under Grace. That is never true as God has already shown us.

Use wisdom, also known as common sense and discernment and judgement that the good Lord gave you, by the Spirit of God. Caution ahead. If discernment does not prevail, chastisement will, unless repentance and mercy steps in first. God has shown us in his word that his commandment to walk in love and maintain good works are still to be done by the letter.

If you don't believe it. Go on. Tempt God. Go break a law of the land and get caught. I promise you, God will not be mocked and as you have tempted the Lord thy God, when he said don't. He will make certain you get understanding real fast after getting those handcuffs put on, and after sitting in that jail cell, and paying many big fines. You will hear the still, small voice behind. It will say. Are you a believer now? Do you now believe that you are to maintain good works of the law, and that you must continue to walk in Love by the letter although I have fulfilled it in you by my Spirit, and that you do not have the license to sin, but you must live holy lives, for I am holy and have made you holy by my Spirit? You are not to tempt me with your foolishness. Good now go and do it. Maintain good works. Walk in love. Walk in fulfillment.

Luke 4:12 And Jesus answering said unto him, It is said, Thou shalt not tempt the Lord thy God.

God knows the heart of every man. God will deal with each man accordingly.

THINGS I'VE LEARNED

CHAPTER 7

●

DISCIPLINE/CHASTISEMENT

Hebrews 12:5-11 And ye have forgotten the exhortation which speaketh unto you as <u>unto children, My son</u>, **despise not thou the chastening of the Lord, nor faint when thou art rebuked of him: For whom the Lord loveth he chasteneth, and scourgeth every son whom he receiveth**. If ye endure chastening, God dealeth with you as with sons; for what son is he whom the father chasteneth not But if ye be without chastisement, whereof all are partakers, then are ye bastards, and not sons. Furthermore we have had fathers of our flesh which corrected *us*, and we gave *them* reverence: shall we not much rather be in subjection unto the Father of spirits, and live For they verily for a few days chastened *us* after their own pleasure; but he for *our* profit, that *we* might be partakers of his holiness. Now no chastening for the present seemeth to be joyous, but grievous: nevertheless afterward it yieldeth the peaceable fruit of righteousness unto them which are exercised thereby.

God desires that we live holy and righteous lives through him. Sin is sin, and God will not tolerate us committing sin. Sin of covetousness, lasciviousness, sexual sins, such as adultery, fornication, homosexuality, bisexuality, stealing, killing, lying, malice, etc. and so forth should be rebuked and corrected and stopped.

The problem is that eating certain meats, not keeping the Sabbath **by the letter**, not bringing the tithe and offering **is not sin**. Society labeled these as sin today because eating certain meats in the bible days were considered sin and not giving tithe was considered sin. These were sins in the days of the law, under Old Covenant, Before Christ, and would bring a curse and even death upon the people if they were not observed since they were the law, and it was by the keeping of the law were the people made righteous and holy before God.

★★★★Today,He has fulfilled all these things. He has shown us that whether you eat certain meat or not is not a sin. We are no better off if we do these things and we are no worse off if we don't do these things by the letter. Just like he took away the inner courts, where only the priest could enter, he has also fulfilled the Sabbath, tithe and offering, atonement money redemption money, etc. He tore the vail down that we no longer have to go through the same ceremonial rituals as they did then. He took away other carnal ordinances such as the bringing of grain, heave, burnt offering, calves, goats, sheep blood and offering, etc. **He became the first fruits, the last/ final offering, the 100%- the best not just 10%,** the cleansing blood, the Passover lamb, the rest, the love, the faith, the grace, the mercy, our righteousness for right standing before our holy God,and he became our way of showing we trust, fear, and honor God. **When we put our faith in his Son Jesus Christ proves this. We have passed the ultimate test, we don't have to prove it anymore, through tithing by the letter, but tithing by the Spirit is required forever. Christ is fulfillment of tithe in the Spirit, showing by, our faith in Jesus, that we have placed God as 1st, and fear and trust and honor God. It is proof eternal that we trust him and that we love him. This is why we are to seek ye 1st the Kingdom of God and his righteous and all things will be added to us. How do we get the kingdom of God and God's righteousness. It is by placing Jesus Christ as head of our life. Putting him first. How do we put him 1st,** by believing in him as Lord and Saviour. It is not by paying tithe by the Letter as of old. <u>The paying of tithe by the letter has been replaced by the fulfillment of tithe in the Spirit by faith in Christ Jesus.</u> Believing in Jesus as the new tithe, the new way of putting God first, is satisfied. It is by Christ we are holy before God forever. Amen.

Read the following:

Hebrews 9:1 Then verily the first covenant had also ordinances of divine service, and a worldly sanctuary. V. 9-11 Which was a figure for the time then present- (only for that present time,-not for our present time) in which were offered both gifts and sacrifices, that could not make him that did the service perfect, as pertaining to the conscience; Which stood only in meats and drinks, and divers washings, and carnal ordinances, imposed on them until the time of reformation. (these things were to be done only for a specified time-until the time of reformation). That means they were to be done until the time Christ came.. v. 11-12 Enter Christ .. But Christ being come .. an high priest of good things to come, by a greater and more perfect tabernacle, not made with hands, that is to say, not of this building. Neither by the blood of goats and calves, but by his own blood he entered once into the holy place, having obtained Eternal redemption for us.

Do you see the issue. We have still been labeling -not tithing- still as a curse and sin as it was under the Law. Christ coming took this carnal ordinance, or regulation, away by fulfilling it. Not tithing is a sin and Not paying a 10% tithe of your income is not a sin. Did you just get confused. Let me clarify. If you are a believer in Christ and do not pay 10% of your income in a tithe, you will not bring a curse on you, and it will not keep the heavens from raining blessings on you, because this not a sin . However, Not receiving the 100% tithe fulfillment through faith in Christ is sin forever. You will bring a curse on you, and it will keep the heavens from raining blessings on you, because it is a sin, for this is blasphemy against the Holy Spirit in not believing in Christ, which is a sin that can not be forgiven if you die in your sins without Christ. It will mean eternal damnation, if you do not believe in Christ and receive his Holy Spirit.

You can keep tithing 10% of your income after you have believed in Christ, there is nothing wrong with that. You can keep preaching and teaching tithing. It is not sin either, because it was law then and the law is never wrong. However, we need to still know the purpose that it served in the tabernacle and the fulfillment by Christ today in our body which is his tabernacle/temple for his dwelling in us today. We need to know Grace over the Law, now . You can stay at the church that teaches on tithing because they are teaching the law. They are not teaching anything wrong, but the teaching that the fulfillment of the tithe and offering is through the THE GRACE of God by faith in Jesus Christ, needs to be heard and shared as well in order for the believer to live no longer under the curses of that old law.

Let us not strive over these issues as they are discussed. Pray for one another's understanding. God is able to make us stand in what is right. We do not have to argue and split churches over these issues. God gave his only begotten Son-Jesus Christ —so we could live no longer under the law-but under his Grace. The law of tithing by the letter is still good, not bad. It just is not the best that Christ has come to bring us into. Again giving is required.

Now if your preacher is teaching you that lying, adultery, homosexuality etc. is not sinning, then you need to pray that God shows him the error of his ways.

Anyone who sin in those things that are truly still considered sin before God, will be dealt with, unless there is repentance and he decides to have mercy, as he did with the city of Ninevah, when Jonah was sent to tell them to repent and turn back to God from their sin or destruction would come. They obeyed God and God was gracious and had mercy on them. This made Jonah mad that God was being forgiving. However, we don't get to tell God what he better do. He alone is God and can choose to have mercy or NOT on whom he chooses. This simply means he can choose not to chastise or to chastise. Our lives are not our own. This does not mean His not showing mercy for a short period of correction means you are doomed to hell or that you have lost fellowship or salvation. No you will know you are still in fellowship with him during your chastisement. You will certainly understand the only way you still here is because of his compassion and mercy are new everyday.

Read the following:

Revelation 3:19 As many as I love, I rebuke and chasten: be zealous therefore, and repent.

Proverbs 3: 11 My son, despise not the chastening of the LORD; neither be weary of his correction:

Hebrews 12:5 And ye have forgotten the exhortation which speaketh unto you as unto children, My son, despise not thou the chastening of the Lord, nor faint when thou art rebuked of him:

Therefore maintain good works in the country and city you live in or you will feel the wrath of the powers (Government/Police) that are ordained by God to deal with you.
If you obey the laws you don't have to worry about the government or the police bothering you, in most cases, if it is not a corrupt or evil system. Sometimes God has other plans, like he had for Joseph, so live by faith and purpose, and the will of God.

Also keep the law not just to keep the government or police from coming after you but so you can live with a good conscience. Knowing you are not doing anything wrong, you can sleep peacefully at night without the worry, fear, stress, hot sweats and high blood pressure coming from a seared conscience.

Just remember any laws of the land or any corruption of those laws from the officiants of such law, that go against God, you are to choose to obey God always, even when it means going against the laws of the land and it's rulers. Remember the 3 Hebrew boys who refused to bow to the idol god that the king had decreed for all to bow to at the sound of the music. Remember Daniel when he would not stop praying to God, even when the king had decreed it. Remember the disciples when they were told not to speak or teach in the Name of Jesus. They said shall we obey God or man. They chose to obey God. We too must always choose to obey God and pray for our elected officials and leaders that they will make laws that are in line with the decrees of our heavenly Father.

God has put these laws in place so we will do good towards one another, and be able to live on earth together in peace. The laws are for US-not for GOD. Yes, God is pleased, when we do as he commands. Whether we choose to do good or bad is really for the benefit of one another. We don't give or take anything from God. It only hurts ourselves and our brother.

CHAPTER 8

●

SUFFERINGS/PERSECUTIONS/AFFLICTIONS/TRIALS/ TRIBULATIONS/IN THE BODY OF CHRIST

So why is there sufferings for God's people if we are no longer cursed. It could be in fact that you are committing one of the sins God has called a sin, and he is disciplining and chastising you to get you back in his will. However, this is not always the case. You may not have done anything. He may just be being faithful. He promised to teach us things about him, and how he operates. He even promises to teach us his ways. The ways he uses are not always ways we approve of. God is faithful, and he is not going to change his plans to demonstrate his power in our lives, to grow us in wisdom, to take us from milk to meat, to help us develop and mature in strength, perserverance and endurance, so he can make us more into his image. That plan is not going to change.He alone is God and we need not forget it.

God told us he is Sovereign. He is God. He is the Potter and we are the Clay. Our lives are not our owns. He can use us as he pleases. We are all parts of his Divine Plan and Purposes. We may not like how he chooses to use us or our loved ones. We may even think God to be a bully at times. Not true.He is just faithful and purposeful in fulfilling his promises to us while fulfilling his purposes in and through us. Again, he is God alone. We are his servants, he is not ours. .

As part of his plans and divine purposes for his chosen, he will allow suffering, and temptation, trials, tribulations and persecutions, into our lives to grow us in our faith, test our faith, to humble us and to prune us so we may produce more fruit, and yes to prove us to see what is truly in our heart, will we keep his commandments or not, even after the divorce, the attack, the betrayal, the loss, etc. He will prove us in order to change us and and prepare us for all that he has planned to use us for. Yes, there will be times that this suffering he allows will have nothing, absolutely nothing to do with him punishing us for sins. He allows suffering into our lives like he allowed it into Job's and Jesus's lives. The devil does nothing without God's permission when we are believers in Christ. You hear oh God does not do evil and wicked to his children. He does allow it for his purposes. He created it for his purposes. He does not tempt us, but he allows temptation from the devil, to teach us to resist it. To teach us to stop lusting for everything and everyone in this world. Things that are fleeting. Stay focused on him and his ways of doing things through all the temptations, and sufferings.

Stop thinking that our God is not just, fair, and righteous if he allows us to experience pain and sufferings. He said we shall share in the fellowship of his sufferings. He said we have been called to suffer as well on his behalf, for his purposes, for his sake, for his glory. At these times, yes we are to pray for deliverance, but if he does not deliver, we must humble ourselves unto God in this time and trust him in it and through it as we continue to obey his instructions daily, while being strengthened by him to endure whatever he may bring forth in our day. This is truly walking by faith and not by sight or the current situation. This is truly denying oneself and picking up our cross and following God no matter what the outcome. We will fear and bless and trust him all the days of our lives on earth, through the good and the bad, knowing he is with us to strengthen us to say yes and endure. We must learn to say, Lord, my will is that you deliver me and rescue me from this, but nevertheless not my will but your will be done. I will humble myself to your will for I know you are with me always to instruct me in this and give me help to bear it. Why do we hear preachers say, God did not send that sickness, or disease, he is a healer. God will allow sickness, disease, and whatever else he chooses to use to bring salvation and eternal life to others. He allowed his Son to be beaten and crucified, killed for a world of many who rejected him. Then he commanded his disciples, us, the believer to follow his same example of submitting to the Father's will with power no matter what so that others may see the manifested works of his love, strength, compassion, grace, mercy, endurance, redemption, restoration, forgiveness and oh so much more in and through us as we obey his voice in every situation daily, no matter how hard and painful it may sometimes be. God does allow some things we do not agree with always.

He allowed Job's ordeal. He allowed Jesus to suffer for us. Jesus told Pilate that he would have no power over him if it had not been given to him by the Father. He used Lazarus for his glory. . He allowed Joseph's brother's to betray him, allowed Potiphar's wife to lie on him, and allowed the butcher to forget about him in jail. He will allow us to go to and through things to bring us to the places of God as Joseph said.

Genesis 50:19-21 And Joseph said unto them, Fear not: for *am* I in the place of God? But as for you, ye thought evil against me; *but* God meant it unto good, to bring to pass, as *it is* this day, to save much people alive. Now therefore fear ye not: I will nourish you, and your little ones. And he comforted them, and spake kindly unto them.

Yes, he loves us. He is a loving Father.

However, we have been created for his glory to be displayed in our lives in and through whatever method or ways he allows. What exactly is his glory. Glory is charateristics of who he is for us, in us, through us, in order to make an impact around us. His Glory is his love, power, strength, forgiveness, grace, mercy, etc.flowing and manifesting Himself to me and the world in every aspect of all things.

This too is why he said we must do the works of he who sent us in his ways, for his ways are not always our ways. The ways he uses often times are not the ways we would have chosen necessarily.

God will allow some things like bitterness to bring us peace. Tears and temptations to humble us.

Read the following:

Isaiah 38:17 Behold, for peace I had great bitterness: but thou hast in love to my soul *delivered it* from the pit of corruption: for thou hast cast all my sins behind thy back.

Acts 20:19 Serving the Lord with all humility of mind, and with many tears, and temptations, which befell me by the lying in wait of the Jews

God is purposeful, just, and righteous in all that he allows to touch our lives.

This is why he tells us in Romans 14 to not judge another man's servant. With us looking on the outside in, the suffering that looks like punishment, chastisement, and discipline just might be God, using this suffering period, as preparation for that person's next season. He brought them this way to humble them, to prune them, to make them stronger, to affect someone else's life through them, so we can all see the power of his resurrection in a person's life after what we thought would be desolation, rubbish, ashes forever. Thanks be to God he is a God that cause rivers in a desert and give beauty from ashes, and life to once dead bones. He is just using them as part of his plan. Just like the disciples were beaten then released. Ezekiel wife died so that the Israelites would watch Ezekiel to see what they are to do when devastation comes on them. They said they counted it a joy to suffer shame for Christ's sake. He uses the good and the bad for his sake. He used Joseph to display a powerful forgiveness story after all that he had been through. He said we too will have some days of suffering, persecutions, trials and tribulations. However, we can be encouraged by the disciples that we can come through it all with God being with us.

Whether we get our will or our way or not. Whether situations and circumstances turn out for the good or bad. Jesus remained faithful till death, so did Stephen. We too are to remain faithful to God till death. However, we think we can turn from God when we have pain in our life, or bad outcomes. No forever is forever. We must do the works of he who sent us even if that work is praying for our enemy while they stone and kill us. He is using us to show faithfulness to him forever. Job suffered, and his friends told him it was something he did or did not do too, but in the end, God told Job's friends neither of them had spoken truth to Job. In other words, their judgment of why Job was going through what he was going through was wrong. Today our judgement of telling people they are going through this and that because they do not tithe by the letter, or that they will go through this or that if they do not tithe by the letter is our making a wrong judgement on God's servant.

***They will go through if they don't tithe by the Spirit for sure. In other words, if you don't put your faith in Christ, you're looking for a life in eternal hell for real.

Read the following scriptures:

John 15:20 Remember the word that I said unto you, The servant is not greater than his lord. If they have persecuted me, they will also persecute you

2 Timothy 3:12 Yea, ALL that will live godly in Christ Jesus shall suffer persecution

Sufferings is part of our growth, part of our building character, strength, patience, endurance, and growing in wisdom, knowledge and faith of God. At times we want to scream at God and not pray to God, when we don't see him. Especially when our tears are streaming and our hearts are shattered, and things are getting worse and worse all around us. It is then we must know that by faith, not by sight, we must walk. Then we understand that though we see and feel one thing what we don't see is that he is with us always, and his power has not diminished, and he is doing a work even with what we see that is all wrong. He is speaking and we must listen to what he is saying in the trial and do what he is speaking at that moment daily obeying his fresh word, his fresh direction and guidance daily that he pours out in overflow daily. See what he is teaching and fulfilling in and through us even in the points of pains in our lives. Learn the valuable lessons being taught even in the dark sessions of life. Let us listen, learn the lessons, apply them, turn from our sins if he tells us there is sin we need to turn from, grow, be an example of pleasing God well in all things, arise and move forward in God, blessing his name, giving him glory and thanks forever.

You will hear one person say, I paid my tithe and things got worse. Another say, I started paying my tithe and things begin to open up. This does not mean one person was blessed and the other person was cursed by God. It only means it is part of their journey, as it is all of our journey. You will hear one person say, I prayed and my loved one still died. I prayed and God healed my loved one. Was God unjust in either of these scenarios. No, he was not.

He is just and righteous in all that he does. This means everything he allows in our lives has a purpose behind it, even if we don't like the ways he does it. Our question is a prayer to God, as to why has this been allowed in our lives and his response may be simply I need you to be a light of endurance and faithfulness in a time like this for those that are watching you in such a time as this, so they will know that the God that strengthened you today will be the same

God that will be able to strengthen them when they face similar if not the same type of situations in life. Can you be that light that I have called and chosen you to be. What will your response to the Lord be. It all is to help us learn of God, to bring us to peace, to cause us to grow in our faith in him, to help us learn how to walk by faith and not by sight, to teach us how to bless him at all times, how to humble ourselves unto him at all times, how to accept good and bad from his hand for his purpose and predetermined will, how to be light and salt in this world, how to do works of he who has sent each of us, and how to keep his commandments and live holy lives, and remain steadfast in our faith, and how to be an example for others of how to live a life of Faith. Thank God for the GRACE that is sufficient to sustain you and I and others in it and grace that will get us all through it.

Oh, how I have learned that God does things in ways that I would not necessarily have chosen for myself or my loved ones to go through, but nevertheless through all his ways he has made me stronger and wiser in the knowledge of who he is, and has shown me many things I had to change in my own character. He has humbled me. Shown me how to walk in humility, by the ways he has taken me.
He has taught us all how to love, forgive, be merciful, show compassion, hold our tongues even when we don't want to. How to be thankful even when everything is falling apart all around us.He has taught us that from being a baby he has carried us all the days of our lives when at many points we felt we were alone and forsaken. You learn that he is your power, peace, and joy. He is your comforter, your strength, your whatever you need him to be –for he is the I AM . You learn in these times how to bless his name always, how to praise him and worship him at all times, through all things. You learn how to suffer for God's sake so that others may gain salvation. You learn how to continue to be about the Father's business even when others still reject his words. You learn to do the works of he who sent you, good, bad, and ugly. You learn to holdfast

to your faith in all things. You learn to be patient-longsuffering. You learn to endure. You learn to obey God always in all things.

He may want to show you, that you will not die if you don't get everything you want. He may have you go through now, so you can encourage your child, or a neighbor, or a loved one, even an enemy, that they can make it too by the Grace of God. We must go to God one on one and ask him Lord what are you up to? He may just say, be still and watch me work. Know that I am God alone, and I am fulfilling Purpose in your life. Obey him. Learn the lesson of waiting, submitting to his will, waiting on his timing, and letting patience have her perfect work. Know that God is the one who changes your seasons in his time. Learn how to remain in rest and peace as your heart is fixed trusting and being still in the Lord.

Read and be encouraged:

Lamentations 3:32-33 But though he cause grief, yet will he have compassion according to the multitude of his mercies. For he doth not afflict willingly nor grieve the children of men.

The above scripture lets us know, God does not willingly afflict his children. Therefore this lets us know that whatever has been allowed has purpose. We may not understand his specific purpose always, but knowing that it has purpose is enough. This is why he told us to Live by faith and not by sight, to set our mind on things above and not beneath, to lean not to our own understanding but Trust him at all times with all our heart and soul. Knowing that even this trial is being used by God for purpose in which He and His Son Jesus may be glorified, in and through our lives. These alone are reasons to rejoice, and rest in God.

He can use us any way he chooses to accomplish His Purposes through our lives. Who are we to say to the one who made us, Why did you make me to use me in this awful way. I don't want to be used in this way. It does not look pretty. It is hard. Others are mocking me, condemning me, judging me and laughing at me. We are the clay and he is the potter. Who can say to the Potter why you make my life to be like this while their life is wealth and riches, with ease and no problems. That can be a wrong judgement as well, because you are going on what you see, but what you may not see is that they are having hardships in other areas that you would not want to deal with? So we shouldn't even judge thinking the grass that looks greener is actually better than our situation. Not necessarily. It is not according to him that runs or willeth, but by him who shows mercy on whom he chooses to show mercy. It means God is in control of all our lives. Our lives are not our own. We may never understand all that God does. We will never agree with the ways he uses. We just want to submit by faith under grace to his perfect will and plan, no matter what the days bring. We are to keep doing good. Don't ever get tired of doing the right thing, even when the wrong things seem to keep happening. Will it be easy? No. Must it be done? Yes.

Even if you are saved, you will still have trials and tribulations in this world. You and I will still suffer for the sake (purposes) of Christ, just like Job, Stephen, and Jesus, and the disciples in the bible. Thanks be to God, Christ is with you and I through every situation. He is through it all to speak to you and strengthen you with his divine nature,as you obey his instructions in every situation, and you will have eternal life with him forever after this current life. Believers are not exempt from bad things and sufferings. We are not guaranteed blessings only and no suffering ever. We will all be afflicted. God is also available to the unbeliever. He still will hear their prayer as they turn their hearts to him, just as he heard each of our prayers.

So, can we please stop scaring people, and telling them they are cursed and suffering, because they did not pay 10% of their income when they are a believer in Christ and are no more under the curse since Grace by Christ has come. We must understand that we must stop condemning the guiltless. God could just be using this suffering in their life for another purpose. Let's encourage them to seek God for his direct answer for why the suffering has come. God will reveal to them what he is doing in their life. He promised to give us wisdom and direction when we ask him anything.

Read Matthew 12:7
But if ye had known what this meaneth, I will have mercy, and not sacrifice, ye would not have **condemn**ed the **guiltless**.

THINGS I'VE LEARNED

JUDGING AND CONDEMNING—ANOTHER MAN'S SERVANT WHEN THAT MAN HAS NOT CONDEMNED HIM

<u>Read Romans Chapter 14:14</u>

Paul was not afraid to say, I do not adhere to the law that certain meats should not be eaten, but to Grace which says nothing is unclean in itself. Paul goes on to say, however, that he was not forcing his opinion and views on anyone who was not as strong as he was. If he did, then he would not be walking in love for his fellow brother, who is not strong in his beliefs as he was.

The difference of opinions on tithing by the letter or not tithing by the letter is the same as this issue on eating or not eating certain meats. We should respect one another and walk in love as Paul shows us here.

We are to still walk in love with those who are weaker in their faith concerning certain things. Paul states, though all things may be ok for him to do, he knows it is not only in his best interest not to do all things, but it is at times in his brother's better interest that he not do certain things, so that his brother will not stumble or fall away, or if it is an unbeliever, that they might be saved, through the love walk shown.

In these verses, Paul goes on to discuss, if your brother or sister is distressed because of what you eat, do not by your eating, destroy someone for whom Christ died. Do not let what you know is good be spoken of as evil. For the kingdom of God is not a matter of eating and drinking, but of righteousness, peace and joy in the Holy Spirit, because anyone who serves Christ in this way is pleasing to God. What Paul was saying here is that no one needs to fall out and be disrespectful and get in strife over these things. If you want to eat pork, eat it, if you don't, don't. What is important is not whether you eat meat or veggies only or a special combination of them both, what matters is are you both Believers in Christ. Neither one of you are sinning. Both of you are to continue to serve the Lord

Many will say this is in regards to meats. Well in Romans 14: 21 where he says **anything** and again in verse 23 where he says **whatsoever you do** . Paul made it clear it was not only regarding meats, but meat, drink, and Anything-tithing included in this anything.

I have spoken to many people who feel they have been condemned and judged by others because they have not been able to pay the tithe according to the letter of law,i.e. 10% of their income, but they are believers in Christ. They have said I have not been able to pay tithes under the old law ways because I have to help my sick parent, or I have to pay for some unexpected family medical debts, or my child has been diagnosed with this illness and the medical bills are piling up, or we both have been laid off and there is no income, or our only income is our unemployment and we are trying to make the ends meet for our family of 5.

Should I be condemned and judged for not paying 10% of my income according to the old letter of the law, or feel that I have sinned or fear I will be cursed, or am I cursed when situations like these arise in my life ? The answer is NO, they should not be condemned and they are not cursed, as we have learned.

Have you ever been afraid to tell someone that you took your tithe to pay your light bill or mortgage, or blessed an elderly parent that needed medical care, fearing they may condemn or judge you, and tell you that you should have paid your tithe first because that is where your blessing is, because it is holy unto the Lord, and commanded by God, and since you didn't, that is why things are not right in your life now, because you have been cursed, and your finances will not ever be right until you pay tithes, and of course they begin to quote Malachi 3 out. I have. Been there. I have been on both ends of the stick, until God taught me better.

The gift I bring to the church house in monetary can be a gift of any amount or percentage to the house of God as he stirs my heart, because as I walk in the house of God I am still bringing my tithe that is in me, fulfilled by the Holy Spirit that dwells in my heart. So see you can pay your bill, bless your parent's and set aside a portion for the church as God leads you in your heart. No more condemnation and curses. My lights and heat are still on to take care of my family in the winter months, and my God used me as a blessing to the church as well.

To many people it doesn't matter that you and your husband both lost your jobs this week, the tithe must be paid regardless by the letter. Forget the mortgage/rent, groceries and heat this winter for your children. Pay those tithe by the letter. Have you ever heard this one? This is a good one. If you don't pay your tithe, on your own, God will cause your car, your refrigerator and your health to fail so that you will have to pay the mechanic, the salesman, and the doctor and guess what? They tithe by the letter. So, they say, God is going to get his tithe one way or the other. And Lord forgive you, if anyone sees that you went on a vacation or have a new purse or shoes. You definitely are on the train bound to chastisement and punishment for not paying 10% and went on a vacation.

See how this has put us in bondage in our minds and spirits. After that conversation, you would think that everything bad that is going on in your life right now is because you didn't pay 10% of your income, tithes by the letter. What about the fact you were a tither faithfully until your husband got sick, before your parent needed special care, before you gave birth to your special needs child. So everything going on in your life is not because you did not pay your 10%. Remember God does not willingly afflict, there is purpose in all that he does. A matter of fact, even our suffering are blessings, when used by God to develop and produce greater things in and through them. He will allow lack and financial distress to touch us to prove to us he is able to provide and sustain us when we trust him, even if you are tither by the letter, every Sunday. Every tither will experience some trial and tribulations while they are in this world. People have you so scared and confused. You just don't know what to do or which way to turn. So now you really depressed, and feel God is not going to help you. You are saying, no one that is a Christian, saved by Grace, say such things, because that is not of God. Well guess what. It is happening. It is being done and you are absolutely right, it is not from God. This is man's judgment and condemnation from wrongly dividing the word according to the law. God would not condemn you for keeping his commandment of taking care of your family even if you had to use the 10% tithe.

Lord Jesus, forgive us, we have messed up your people badly. Live in Grace. Christ has set you free. He came to set the captives free. God did not come to place us in bondage. He came to set us free and then he tells us do not again be entangled in bondage by anyone, for you have indeed been set free by the SON.

Read the following scriptures.
★★★

Acts 5:29 Then Peter and the other apostles answered and said, We ought to obey God rather than men.

1 Timothy 5:4 But if any widow have children or nephews, let them learn first to shew **piety** at home, and to requite their parents: for that is good and acceptable before God.

Piety definition: reverence for God or fulfillment of religious obligations

1 Timothy 5:8 – But if any provide not for his own, and specially for those of his own house, he hath denied the faith, and is worst than an infidel.

You just read scriptures speaking that we must obey God not man, and that a person is worse than an infidel if they do not take care of their family. Taking care of one's family is also a commandment of God's. They did not sin, and should not feel guilty or condemned and judged by man. Notice again, I said condemned by man, not by God. This is why we must focus on what God is saying and not man.

Leave people be. Walk in the things that you agree on while striving to do all God has called each of you to do. Let God be God. Both of you should be striving to please God. If there is a point or issue that you disagree on. God, is able to make his servant stand. If you are wrong, he is able to show you, just as he is able to show the other. Walk in love always. This is what the following scripture says.

<u>Phillippians 3:14-16</u> I press toward the mark for the prize of the high calling of God in Christ Jesus. **Let us therefore, as many as be perfect, be thus minded: and if in anything ye be otherwise minded, God shall reveal even this unto you. Nevertheless, whereto we have already attained, let us walk by the same rule, let us mind the same thing.**

Discuss but do not strive with one another.

Tithing 10% is not a right or wrong, sin or not sin issue, which we have made it to be. It is a law and grace and weaker or stronger faith situation, and a by the letter or by the Spirit issue. In other words it is a understanding of his word on this topic. That understanding cometh from God. He is always here to give us understanding. This is why he has ordained this book. Blessings.

In other words paying 10% of your income is not a sin. Not paying 10% of your income is not a sin. Not believing in Christ, not putting your faith in him, The Son of God, our Lord and Saviour, is a sin. For it is in your believing and placing your faith in Christ only that fulfills all the laws by Grace.

This law is not a law that was meant to be continually kept by the letter after Christ came. Just as keeping the Sabbath day according to the law was not meant to be kept by the letter, which is what Jesus was demonstrating when he was in the field with the disciples and healing the lame man on the Sabbath. Jesus said I am the Sabbath. He is the tithe. Jesus was proving to us-in him is the fulfillment of the Sabbath, tithes, and so much more. We must begin to live according to Grace and the Spirit not continue to condemn the guiltless when they choose not to give 10% of their income. God is still able to move our hearts to give whatever he desires us to give. It can be 10% or less, or much more. All is generous giving when it is in obedience to our God.

THINGS I'VE LEARNED

CHAPTER 10

SELF CONDEMNATION

In the following scriptures the issue of self condemnation is addressed.

Romans 14:5-6 One man esteemeth one day above another: another esteemeth every day *alike*. Let every man be fully persuaded in his own mind. He that regardeth the day, regardeth *it* unto the Lord; and he that regardeth not the day, to the Lord he doth not regard *it*. He that eateth, eateth to the Lord, for he giveth God thanks; and he that eateth not, to the Lord he eateth not, and giveth God thanks For none of us liveth to himself, and no man dieth to himself

Romans 14: v.22-23
Hast thou faith? Have it to thyself before God. Happy is he that condemneth not himself in that thing which he alloweth. And he that doubteth is damned if he eat, because he eateth not of faith: for whatsoever is not of faith is sin.

God said if you don't believe you should stop tithing by the letter. That is fine. You are not sinning. You don't have to stop tithing by the letter just because you are learning better. See as we grow, we sometimes hear things as weaker Christians in a particular area and we don't have our faith built up in that area yet. So, you prefer to continue to do what you have been doing .. As long as it is not sin. God is fine with that, for you know you are doing it unto him. He will grow your faith in this area at his pace. This is not a follow the leader Gospel after we become believers. We all grow at different paces. This is why he wants us to respect one another in our growth. We, means everyone, including pastors, leaders, teachers, evangelists, congregation member, every disciple. We have to give grace and understanding for our pastors, teachers, and leaders, that they too are still learning and growing in their understanding of Grace daily. They have been called and chosen, but have not learned everything they need to know. We all must extend this grace to one another as we all grow in the grace and wisdom of Christ as his word says and understand let us come alongside one another and exhort and edify one another as we all are renewed in our mind and become willing and obedient to walk in the newness of spirit and understanding from our God.

We will always have babes and more mature, weaker and stronger Christians in this life. Some members may be stronger in an area of Grace than some Pastors. We all are here to not to become bitter but to pray for one another as we all continue to grow . God is God. He will show us clearly what he is speaking in his word to each of us individually. He will not keep any of us in confusion. He is not a God that authors confusion. He is able to clear up every thing, every issue we are confused about. We are here to help one another and be patient with one another in love.

He does not want us to self condemn ourselves either by doing a follow the leader gospel. If you don't want to change something right now, because you don't think it is the right thing to do. That is fine. Go to God in prayer and ask him to help you understand and he will. He is a patient God. Walk in what you are strong in right now. If you don't and you do something that you in your own heart don't feel is right, and it bothers your conscience, but you do it anyhow because I say so, or your mom, or dad, or friend says so, but you don't have your faith built to that point to believe in your own heart that it is so, you will feel guilty after doing it because your heart did not believe it for yourself. You were just following what I or others said.

You will lose your peace. God wants you to follow the things that leave you in peace. The Spirit of God is able to lead you into that Peace, his perfect peace regarding every topic. While reading this book, after reading this book, Pray to God to show you his perfect understanding and give you his perfect peace pertaining to this topic.

*Romans 14:19- Let us therefore follow after the things which make for peace, and things wherewith one may edify another.

When you do things that take your peace, even if they were the right thing, you start saying I should not have done that,because your faith is weaker in that area. You now have brought self condemnation. This means you are having feelings of guilt and condemnation. Again it is not condemnation from God but from yourself. You will feel disapproval before God and feel guilty before God, whenever you do something that you know is not sin but still don't feel right doing. Whenever you do something you feel is not right in your own heart, it is sin for you, even if it is not considered sin before God. So, follow after the things in faith you are strong in. Then whatsoever you do in faith towards God from your heart, you will be pleased and so will God.

You may ask if it is not sin, why would I feel guilty in doing it. Because when we are use to doing things for so long from generations to generations for years, and God comes to renew our minds, our flesh automatically wants to reject it. It does not want to be reprogrammed or renewed as the Spirit is leading, so our flesh rejects the Spirits teaching. It does not want to accept the change for what ever reason. Mom and Dad will not understand. I don't want to upset them, etc. These are typical struggles we will go through as God teaches and conforms us to his thinking. Continue to pray and seek God's face on every subject, and trust him to guide you into all his truth at your pace. Continue to grow at your own pace in God. Be blessed. Understand that you will eventually have to put away your way and guilt and self condemnation for God's renewing ways and his word in order to grow and mature from the old to new in Christ. We must grow from the milk to the meat. We must grow from faith to faith and from glory to glory. Every round is taking us higher in him. This means we must grow up. Grow up in Christ and our understanding of his word in our lives.

THINGS I'VE LEARNED

●

CHAPTER 11

DO NOT STRIVE

To Tithe by the letter or Not to Tithe by the letter, Should not be an issue for The Body of Christ to be in War about. We should not be in Strife/Argument/and Bitterness over this Issue.

Tithing is still Required. It is just no longer required by the letter as it was under the Law, it is now required by the fulfillment through the Holy Spirit. So Tithing is still REQUIRED.

Christ satisfied that carnal ordinance of tithing by the letter. If you want to still give 10% notice I said Give not tithe. Giving and tithing are different. Giving 10% or less or more is still Required. Giving 10% is not mandatory. Giving is still required under Grace. Giving freely with a bountiful heart, cheerfully, as God stirs your heart today, without the curse, and with all the blessings and promises, to reap bountifully from a bountiful heart giving –that is GRACE.

We understand there will be times we will always have to correct, rebuke, bring to someone's attention their sin or wrong behavior, and others will have to do the same with us., etc. We are commanded to do so in love and with meekness, because it could be us who fall into the same thing tomorrow.

So we know correction is needed in the Body of Christ. Strife is not.

We in the body of Christ have made the issue not tithing 10% an issue to be in strife over. Exactly what the enemy wants. However, God said the carnal ordinance of tithing by the letter was fulfilled by the Spirit with the coming of Christ. So, don't get in strife over these things any longer.

So, in conclusion, When we discuss issues like the tithe and meats and celebrations of Christ, we can discuss it without striving amongst believers or unbelievers. We still are not to judge harshly, condemn, argue, or get in strife. We are to leave one another in God's hands, and pray for each other, while having good conversations in love that may be a conversation with rebuke and correction seasoned with grace and love. This is what Jesus demonstrated when he corrected the woman caught in adultry. He corrected her in love with grace and mercy. Unlike the men who wanted to correct her with strife and condemnation. Always, Always choose the path of walking in LOVE.

With all that God has taught us. Let us not strive but walk in agreement on the things that we agree on. Amen.

Read the following:

★Phillippians 3:15 Let us therefore, as many be perfect, be thus minded: and if in anything ye be otherwise minded,---God shall reveal even this unto you. Nevertheless, whereto we have already attained, let us walk by the same rule, let us mind the same thing.

★Titus 3:2-9 To speak evil of no man, to be no brawlers, but gentle, shewing all meekness unto all men. For we ourselves also were sometimes foolish, disobedient, deceived, serving divers lusts, and pleasures, living in malice and envy, hateful, and hating one another. But after that the kindness and love of God our Saviour toward man appeared, Not by works of righteousness which we have done, but according to his mercy he saved us, by the washing of regeneration, and renewing of the Holy Ghost; which he shed on us abundantly through Jesus Christ our Saviour; That being justified by his grace, we should be made heirs according to the hope of eternal life. This is a faithful saying, and these things I will that thou affirm constantly, that they which have believed in God might be careful to maintain good works. These things are good and profitable unto men. But avoid foolish questions and genealogies, and contentions, and strivings about the law; for they are unprofitable and vain.

THINGS I'VE LEARNED

●

CHAPTER 12

●

DON'T WALK IN PRIDE/SHAME/GUILT

Humble yourself under the mighty hand of God in obedience to him as a child and continue to Grow in the Grace that is in Christ Jesus.

Don't be afraid to admit you have been teaching the law as it had been taught to you. **Through the traditional teaching, I had been taught that I had to tithe by the letter or be cursed. This is what was passed through generations. This was all I knew. I taught this as a biblical teacher of the word as well.**

I admit it. Guilty as charged. I was never taught the fulfillment of the tithe by the Holy Spirit in me by Grace and Faith in my Lord Jesus Christ. I was never taught that paying tithe by the letter is not required but that Giving, whether 1% or 5% or 10% or 50% etc. was still required. I was not taught that Tithe and regular giving are different.

Thank God for his Grace. I can teach it correctly now that he has given me understanding.

<u>Don't worry about what others are going to say-that is pride, fear, and approval addiction from men rearing. If God is for you. That is enough.</u>

Pride fears man and does not fear God. Fear God at all times.

Proverbs 16:18- Pride *goeth* before destruction, and an haughty spirit before a fall

Matthew 10:26-28 Fear them not therefore: for there is nothing covered, that shall not be revealed; and hid, that shall not be known. What I tell you in darkness, *that* speak ye in light: and what ye hear in the ear, *that* preach ye upon the housetops. And fear not them which kill the body, but are not able to kill the soul: but rather fear him which is able to destroy both soul and body in hell.

Do not be offended-correct your actions-No longer walk with blind folds to this truth of Grace-by Christ

Matthew 15:12-13 Then came his disciples, and said unto him, Knowest thou that the Pharisees were offended, after they heard this saying? But he answered and said, Every plant, which my heavenly Father hath not planted, shall be rooted up. Let them alone: they be blind leaders of the blind. And if the blind lead the blind, both shall fall into the ditch.

Another important question is -Should tithing be taught in the church?

****The following scriptures command we are to learn the word of God from the leaders, and teachers he directs us to. We are also to take the word taught and study with prayer to God in our own personal study time where he will teach us how to rightly divide the word of truth for ourselves, so that we may not be deceived by others or our own misunderstanding, or enticements from the devil to lead us away from truth or of some traditional teaching.**

2 Timothy 4:1-2 I charge thee therefore before God, and the Lord Jesus Christ, who shall judge the quick and the dead at his appearing and his kingdom. **Preach the word**; be in season, out of season; reprove, rebuke, exhort with all longsuffering and doctrine.

1 Timothy 4:11-12 These things command and **teach**. Let no man despise thy youth; but be thou an example of the believers, in word, in conversation, in charity, in spirit,in faith, in purity.

Teaching about tithing is needed. We need to understand its' meaning and purpose in the Old Tabernacle, in order to appreciate The Saviour, Jesus Christ, fulfillment of it

Therefore Yes, tithing and offering should be taught.

The law of tithing is still good. The law is not sin. Wherefore the law is holy, and the commandment holy, and just, and good, a better has come, a greater has come. His name – JESUS, fulling the law.

It is like this. A car made today is better than a car made 60 years ago, it is better than a horse and buggy years ago. The horse and buggy can still be used today to go to work. Nothing would be wrong with that. However, better has come. Better forms of transportation are available to us today. So the same is with the law of tithe. It is still good. It can still be done. You can still live under the curse of the law if you do not obey the law of tithe. However, better has come. His name is Jesus Christ, therefore today we can give as the Lord stirs each of our heart any percentage, without being any longer under the curse of the Law. This is the Grace of God through Faith in his Son Jesus Christ. Glory to God.

He has satisfied the law/ordinance of paying tithe and offering as in the old tabernacle and under the old covenant as we have already discussed.

He also has satisfied the law of giving but he still commands Giving to be done by the letter in the same way he commands us to by the letter continue not to steal, kill, and lie.

Remember Tithe by the letter under the law was a mandatory 10%. In our Giving under Grace. There is not a set percentage.

Read his commandments about giving below. They do not mandate a 10%. Therefore, your giving can be 10%, 100%, or 1% or 3%., or more. No more curses, No more bondages. Liberty in giving because the tithe and offering, and the atonement money, and the redemption money, and other offerings have been satisfied already by Jesus in us. So when I come into the house of God, I am walking in with my Tithe fulfilled and with my giving gift in my hand. Both being fulfilled. Glory to God.

2 Corinthians 9:7 Every man according **as he purposeth in his heart,** *so let him give*; not grudgingly, or of necessity: **for God loveth a cheerful giver.**

1 Corinthians 16:2 Upon the first day of the **week** let every one of you **lay** by him in store, as God hath prospered him, that there be no gatherings when I come.

Luke 6:38 Give, and it shall be given unto you; good measure, pressed down, **and** shaken together, **and** running over, **shall** men **give** into your bosom. For with the same measure that ye mete withal **it shall be** measured to you again.

THINGS I'VE LEARNED

CHAPTER 13

●

GIVING IS STILL COMMANDED BY GOD-YOU CAN'T GET AWAY FROM IT

As discussed, previously, there is no set percentage now to give. God has set us free from the set percentage. He has become the full 100% tithe and offering . His body and his blood was more than 10% tithe and offering He says now give not because the law is demanding it (i.e . not grudgingly or of necessity) but give whatever you purposed in your heart to give, because that is the amount you are giving with a bountiful and cheerful, and generous heart not a grudging heart as you did under the law. He has set us free from the percentage, from the bondage.

I love too how he still shows us it is still connected to OUR HEART and guess who is in control of our heart, and guess who dwells in the heart of every believer, and guess where the laws of God are written-on our heart, no longer on tablets in the days of Moses.

We are not in control of ourselves. God is in control. Our hearts are in his hand. He can turn our hearts any way he pleases, causing us to give whatever he pleases, whenever he pleases, no matter what our current situations are. If he says give 50% today. That is what you do no matter what else is going on. If he says it. Do it. But if he says just give this and go do this with that amount. Do that. It is all about being

directed and guided by the Holy Spirit in this area as well as in every area of our lives. Amen to that.

Read :

We are not our own.

1 Corinthians 6:19 -20 What? know ye not that your body is the temple of the Holy Ghost *which is* in you, which ye have of God, and ye are not your own? For ye are bought with a price: therefore glorify God in your body, and in your spirit, which are God's.

Our hearts are in the Lord's hand
Proverbs 21:1 The king's heart is in the hand of the LORD, as the rivers of water: he turneth it whithersoever he will.

In Exodus 36:2-7 L ook at this he stirred up hearts that gave and it ended up being more than enough that Moses had to tell the people to stop. God is still the same. He can stir up our hearts today in the same way in giving.

Hebrews 13:8 Jesus Christ the same yesterday, and today, and for ever.

Again, I say, what was that about, you were not going to do what? You were not going to give any money to the church? Yes, that is what I thought you said. Well guess what, We are not in control of anything when God takes a hold of us.

So the church, and the preachers, and the workers, and anybody who thought, if the people do not tithe by the letter, the doors of the church will close, the lights will be turned off, and the roof will fall in.

No worries. He still commands us to Give. He will bless. He is in control of our hearts and able to stir them to give above and beyond anything we can ask or think.

So often **2 Corinthians 9:5-8** is taught with the emphasis on sowing sparingly and reaping sparingly and sowing bountifully and reaping bountifully. Meaning the less you give the smaller your reward will be that you receive from God, and the more you give the more you will receive from God. When actually God's emphasis is not that at all. His focus is not the amount/quantity given. His focus is on the quality of your giving. Is it sown from a cheerful and bountiful heart? Whether the amount is big or small. God knows our heart and he responds to the heart he knows is giving it cheerfully, not resenting it, not reluctant, not feeling you have to do it, but because you want to do it. Not out of pride as the Pharisee that stood there bragging about himself and downing the other man, and not because you are bound by the law.

You want to be a blessing and you want to see the faithfulness of God's grace. So, give whatever quantity that God stirs your heart to give with the quality of a bountiful Heart and reap bountifully from your bountiful heart giving from your more than able God. Know that God is still in the multiplying business today like he was with 5 loaves and 2 fish.

Be a Blessing--Genesis 12:2 And I will make of thee a great nation, and I will bless thee, and make thy name great; and thou shalt be a blessing

To be able to give is a blessing. To give is a good work. To give is worship to a great heavenly Father. An amazing God.

You and I will always have to give to the Body of Christ, to His works and to his people. You cannot escape giving nor ever think you do not have to give to the Body of Christ.

God does not need our money. However, he does work through us to use our giving to bless others, as he has commanded us to do.

Give to be a blessing to your church and others in and outside the church, to pay for the upkeep of the church and the bills of the church so that you can have a nice place to come and gather with other believers forsaking not the assembling of ourselves as God commanded. We don't want leaky roofs, and benches falling apart, and patched windows and walls. We want to be a blessing to the house of God. We want to bless the household of faith. We want to pay the workers of the church —pastors, janitors, musicians, secretaries, etc. they are due their honor, even if they still work other jobs as Paul the apostle did. We also want the church we attend to be able to be a blessing to their members if a need arises and to the community and around the world. In order for our church to do this, it requires we give money, time, and other resources as well.

Read:

Acts 20:35 I have shewed you all things, how that so labouring ye ought to support the weak, and to remember the words of the Lord Jesus, how he said, It is more blessed to give than to receive

Galatians 6:9-10 And let us not be weary in well doing: for in due season we shall reap, if we faint not. As we have therefore opportunity, **let us do good unto all *men*, especially unto them who are of the household of faith.**

1 Timothy 5:17-18 Let the elders that rule well be counted worthy of double honour, especially they who labour in the word and doctrine. For the scripture saith, Thou shalt not muzzle the ox that treadeth out the corn. And, The labourer *is* worthy of his reward.

Everything we have has been given to us by God.

1 Corinthians 4:7 For who maketh thee to differ *from another*? and what hast thou that thou didst not receive? now if thou didst receive *it*, why dost thou glory, as if thou hadst not received *it*?

You will lose the argument over Giving of anything, time, money, food, etc. and of any percentage. Giving is required. Do not try to mock God thinking well I can give time but I will never give money. God said we are not our own. This life we live are not ours. We have been bought with a price. We are his servants. We were created to do His will, not ours. We were created to give him glory, and do the works he predestined for us to do.

Many will say, but why would I not want to give 10% when he has blessed me and tells me the other 90% is mine. Why can I not give him a dime out of every dollar when he has given me so much. Why can I not be generous as he commanded me and give the 10%. If I don't pay tithes that proves I don't trust God with my life and money. That proves I am not being obedient and will be cursed. That proves I am trusting me more than God or I am trusting my money more than God, or I say I am walking by faith, but I am really walking by fear. Also, another one I have heard is, if I don't pay tithes that proves I don't have faith in God, and that I am not willing to put God 1st.

All of these statements sound so honorable and right before God, but really they are only condemning God's people because we don't understand truth. These statements are not biblical. They sound like truth with good reasoning. They sound so honorable unto the Lord. They however are not truth. They are all condemnation statements that we have made honorable, not realizing we are condemning with them.

It is condemning to his people and causing his people to live in the bondage of the Law and not under the Grace he has provided for his children.

The following is truth.

When you present yourself, your 100% body, you, your life, as a living sacrifice to God by placing faith in Jesus Christ, and his Holy Spirit comes to make his abode in you, that is the best giving, the best offering and sacrifice you could give him in return for all his goodness. It is the fulfillment of the tithe and all the law. Your 100% dedication of your life to him for all the goodness he has done for you and given to you, is better than the dime you could give out of every dollar. It is more generous than the 10% you could put in the offering plate in giving. It means I have totally put my trust in God. I am not living by fear but trust at all times. I have faith in Jesus. My faith in Jesus is proof of my trust in God. Does God test our faith? Does he prove us? Yes, he does, but it is not by telling us to do things by the letter that he no longer requires to be done by the letter anymore. He does not prove us by telling us to bring atonement and redemption money or sprinkle blood around the doorpost, or bring the grain and heave offering. He may test us with financial challenges to see if we will trust him to provide according to our faith and not according to our works of the law, therefore we don't need to pay a tithe by the letter to get a financial blessing when we have all blessings and promises in Christ Jesus. He may prove us in our health to see will we hold on to our faith even when our health is failing. Are we understanding. My life is the best and most generous thing, sacrifice, and offering, that I can give to God for all his goodness. Give God glory.

We proved to him our love, faith, and trust in him when we believed in Christ. We put him 1ˢᵗ when we believed in his 1ˢᵗ born Son- Jesus Christ. That was finished. How does God see I trust him? By his Holy Spirit given as his seal on our lives. Now I still must maintain good works according to the laws of love towards one another and do and go where he sends us to be a light in this world.

Do not strive with one another over this and though this may be one of those things hard to understand or receive from God. It is still his TRUTH. It is still his GRACE.

THINGS I'VE LEARNED

●

_____

_____

_____

_____

_____

_____

_____

_____

_____

_____

_____

_____

_____

_____

_____

_____

_____

_____

_____

_____

_____

_____

_____

_____

TEACH FULFILLMENT OF THE LAW BY GRACE THROUGH FAITH IN CHRIST

Pastors and teachers, if we want to teach about tithe and offering, teach the history of it in order to bring us to fulfillment by Christ of them by Grace. Do not teach as something to be continued by the letter, but as something fulfilled and continued by and through the Holy Spirit through Jesus Christ.

<u>Read the following scriptures:</u>

<u>John 1:17</u> For the law was given by Moses but grace and truth came by Jesus Christ.

<u>John 8:36</u> If the Son therefore shall make you free, you shall be free indeed

<u>Romans 3:28</u> Therefore we conclude that man is justified by faith, without the deeds of the law, through the redemption that is in Christ Jesus.

<u>Galatians 3:24-25</u>- Wherefore the law was our schoolmaster *to bring us* unto Christ, that we might be justified by faith. But after that faith is come, we are no longer under a schoolmaster.

<u>Matthew 5:17-20</u> Think not that I am come to destroy the law, or the prophets: I am not come to destroy, but to fulfil. For verily I say unto you, Till heaven and earth pass, one jot or one tittle shall in no wise pass from the law, till all be fulfilled. Whosoever therefore shall break one of these least commandments, and shall teach men so, he shall be called the least in the kingdom of heaven: but whosoever shall do and teach *them*, the same shall be called great in the kingdom of heaven For I say unto you, That except your righteousness shall exceed *the righteousness* of the scribes and Pharisees, ye shall in no case enter into the kingdom of heaven.

So often Matthew 5:17-20 has been used by others to say, see this scripture says we are to keep all the laws by the letter, each and every one, or they say, see we are to keep all the laws, the only difference is that now we have his Holy Spirit, in us, to help us do each one by the letter. They also use this scripture to condemn teachers that are teaching correctly that we are no longer under Mosaic Laws but under Grace. They say that these teachers are breaking the law and teaching others to break the law as well. This is incorrect.

We as teachers of the gospel must be certain that we teach others to keep the law, not break the law.

Therefore, as teachers, we now must teach that in order for anyone to actually keep or fulfill the law and not break the law themselves they have to believe in the one who has already completed this for us, and that is believe on Christ. Christ is the end of righteousness under the Law. Faith in Christ is the only way we keep the Law.

This is why he said to the Pharisees and the people unless their righteousness exceeds the righteousness of the scribes and Pharisees, they WOULD NOT enter into the KINGDOM OF HEAVEN.

What was the righteousness of the Pharisees and Sadducees based on? MOSAIC LAW-the righteousness of the Law by the letter.

There was an exceeding greater Righteousness than the Law now available-HIS NAME-JESUS CHRIST, and the Pharisees and Sadducees were rejecting Jesus-the LAW.

Christ was making this plain. If we read on through verses 21-48 we would have discovered, how plain he was making it to us. Christ was teaching them they could not keep the law. He told them of old-that which the Mosaic law stated as part of the old covenant, then he paralleled it with what the new Covenant-which was Him-Christ-said they must do if they wanted to live by not only the law but the lawgiver/lawmaker himself, and if they adhered to the Mosaic law of old and not to what he was saying they would be guilty of breaking the law, and in danger of judgment or punishment. However if they accepted him as Saviour they then fulfill his law. He was trying to teach them accept me as Lord over your life and then you have fulfilled the law in the way I now require, and then you can escape judgement.

See Christ was pretty much saying there is a new Sherriff (Covenant in town) and what the old said is fulfilled by the new. Christ is saying, listen to me the New and do what I the New Covenant is telling you to do. If you don't listen to me, you are in danger of hell fire, because the old Mosaic Law won't save you now.

And once you are saved don't revert back to trying to keep the Mosaic laws to keep your right standing. This is what happened in Acts 15: 1-35, and this was addressed also in Galatians Chapter 3. It is finished in Christ.

Let's look at the following verses:

Matthew v.21-26 -deal with Murder —You have heard that it was said by them of old time, Thou shall not kill, and whosoever shall kill shall be in danger of judgement

But I say unto you, That whosoever is angry with his brother without a cause shall be in danger of the judgement, and whosoever shall say to his brother Raca shall be in danger of the council; but whoso ever shall say thou fool, shall be in danger of hell fire.

How many times, I wonder had the Pharisees gotten angry with their brother over silly things, or called someone a fool. How many times have you? They did not have to murder or kill anyone, they only had to say fool.

v.27-30-deal with adultery- Ye have heard that it was said by them of old time, Thou shalt not commit adultery: But I say unto you, That whosoever looketh on a woman to lust after her committeth adultery with her already in his heart. And if thy right eye offend thee pluck it out and cast it from thee: for it is profitable for thee that one of thy members should perish, and not that thy whole body should be cast into hell. And if thy right hand offend thee, cut it off, and cast it from thee

How many times, I wonder had the Pharisees looked on a woman and lusted after her in their heart, although they never acted on it? How many times have you lusted after the opposite sex in your heart?

I don't see too many one eyed and one armed men and women walking around today. Why is that? Because in this area of adultery they quickly recognize the benefit of living under Grace and not under the Law. They don't teach this about the law of adultery and the consequences or curses of becoming one eyed and one armed. They don't maintain this law, but they quickly say, oh the law of tithing by the letter must be maintained. If you break one law you break them all remember. I didn't say it. Christ did. I am only the messenger.

v.31-48 Christ continues on with areas of making oaths (v. 33-37), an eye for an eye (v.38-42)
Love for enemies (v 43-48)

The point Christ was showing them was they were not keeping his laws. To obey him-was easy- believe in him. If they wanted to live by the Law, he threw in a few added restrictions to see just how enticing living under the bondage of the law would continue to be. After all he was God, he could tact on extra restrictions, right there on the spot and he did. It is virtually impossible to live under the law as Christ demonstrated. Just believe on Christ as Lord and Saviour and live in his blessings while maintaining good works and walking in love with one another.

Salvation and Right standing-Righteousness before God comes ONLY by Christ now. Not by how well you are keeping or have kept the law. Read the following

John 3:3 Jesus answered and said unto him, Verily, verily, I say unto thee, **Except a man be born again, he cannot see the kingdom of God.**

It did not matter how many laws the Pharisees and Sadducees kept, it did not matter how much in tithe and offering they brought to the temple, they still would not see the kingdom of God. They would be condemned to hell in the last days, if they rejected our Lord and Saviour Jesus Christ, and many still rejected Christ insisting on the Mosaic laws to save and keep them in right standing.

Read:

Romans 3:20-31 Therefore by the deeds of the law there shall no flesh be justified in his sight: for by the law *is* the knowledge of sin. **But now the righteousness of God without the law is manifested,** being witnessed by the law and the prophets; **Even the righteousness of God *which is* by faith of Jesus Christ unto all and upon all them that believe:** for there is no difference: For all have sinned, and come short of the glory of God Being justified freely by his grace through the redemption that is in Christ Jesus

Whom God hath set forth *to be* a propitiation through faith in his blood, to declare his righteousness for the remission of sins that are past, through the forbearance of God; To declare, *I say*, at this time his righteousness: that he might be just, and the justifier of him which believeth in Jesus. Where *is* boasting then? It is excluded. By what law? of works? Nay: but by the law of faith. Therefore we conclude that a man is justified by faith without the deeds of the law. *Is he* the God of the Jews only? *is he* not also of the Gentiles? Yes, of the Gentiles also: Seeing *it is* one God, which shall justify the circumcision by faith, and uncircumcision through faith.

Do we then make void the law through faith? God forbid: yea, we establish the law.

In Romans 2:26-29, he was showing the Jews and the Gentiles, using circumcision as an example, that if the Gentiles (who were the uncircumcision), who were not under the law-meaning they did not have to be circumcised- believed in Christ, they have kept the righteousness of the law, and the Gentile is now considered right before God, without being circumcised by the letter, but being circumcised in the heart, by the Spirit, by believing in Christ alone, without the letter of circumcision.

He also said the Jews, who were under the law, who had to be circumcised according to the law-If the Jews got circumcised by the letter and did not believe on Jesus, they had not kept the righteousness of the law, and were not considered in right standing before God any longer by their circumcision by the letter.

Therefore the Jews keeping the letter of the law-through circumcision, are at the same time, transgressing the law, because they did not believe in Christ and receive fulfillment of the law in their hearts by the Spirit.

But the Gentiles, believing in Christ alone, without being circumcised, without keeping the letter of the law, but believing in

Christ and receiving his Spirit in their hearts, have fulfilled the law in themselves, and is viewed as a Jew would be-acceptable before God, not because he kept the law of circumcision by the letter but he has fulfilled the law by the Spirit, that says believe in Christ and receive the Holy Spirit in your heart, thereby all the laws are written and fulfilled in your heart.

THINGS I'VE LEARNED

CHAPTER 15

●

LET'S LOOK CLOSER AT WHAT JESUS HAS FULFILLED

Let's continue:

The biggest things we have to understand are:

1. We must understand there were ordinances under the Old Covenant for the Old Tabernacle that had to be observed for the people to be holy before the Lord.
2. We must understand there is now a New Covenant with a New Tabernacle.
3. We must understand there is an Old Priesthood and a New Priesthood
4. We must understand there were Laws/Ordinances that were specifically for the Tabernacle and there were Laws of the Land under the government that was separate from the Tabernacle Laws, but were connected.

There is an **Old Tabernacle and a New Tabernacle, and the things that were required regarding the Old Tabernacle was a foreshadow of Christ who would come and have been fulfilled by Christ's coming. Those carnal ordinances, etc. are no longer required, no longer needed by the letter for the New Tabernacle. They are fulfilled by Christ in the New Covenant as the New Tabernacle was brought forth.**

Let's get understanding of some comparision between the Old and the New Tabernacle

Read the following scriptures:

Exodus chapters 25 thru Chapter 28 describes the building of the Old Tabernacle and the requirements.

Hebrews Chapter 9 and 10 Speaks about the Old Covenant and Old Tabernacle the New Tabernacle and the New Covenant.

The purpose of the Laws and Regulations of the Old Covenant and Old Tabernacle were they would show us our sins and our sinful state that we might turn to Christ, whom alone, being our redeemer, and Saviour, would be able to deliver us from all the bondage and curses of sin forever.

Read the following:

Galatians 3:24-25 Wherefore the law was our schoolmaster *to bring us* unto Christ, that we might be justified by faith. But after that faith is come, we are no longer under a schoolmaster.

However, today in many churches we are still teaching that After Christ, and the New tabernacle and New covenant have come, that we still must keep the carnal ordinances of the Old Tabernacle and of the Old Covenant, such as bringing tithe and offerings, observing Sabbaths, observing various washings, etc. Many teach that we should not break the Sabbath, no work should be done, we should rest on this day, not understanding Christ is now our Sabbath. He became our entry into rest now and for eternity. When we believe on him as Lord and Saviour we enter this rest forever. Many keep the various washings, and observances of not eating certain meats and moon festivals, Passover etc. They keep these things by the letter.

Christ coming said he fulfilled these cardinal ordinances..

All these Cardinal ordinances were given to the Israelites after God delivered them from their place of bondage- Egypt using Moses and Aaron as their leaders. The Israelites were to keep these laws, celebrations, observances as a rememberance of what God had done for them in bringing them out of their bitter bondage. These things were to be done forever. Yes, forever.

Now, Christ has fulfilled them in each believer thereby having them forever observed and forever fulfilled by the Spirit of Christ in each believer.

***His commandment that they must be kept forever has not changed. His method of how they would be kept forever has changed. Changed from the Law to Grace. Changed from by the Letter to through the receiving of the Holy Spirit into your heart by believing in the Son of God, Jesus Christ.**

Read also the following scriptures:

Hebrews 9:8-11 Stood only in carnal ordinances, meats, and drinks and various washings and tithe and offereing, do not eat this or that, do not touch this or that. All of these things were imposed on them until reformation (until Christ came) ..Read this whole chapter.

Hebrews 7 Discusses a change of priesthood, a change of law.

Let's discuss the following things of the Old Tabernacle in relation to Christ— the Fulfillment.

The Old tabernacle building was designed to foreshadow the coming of our Messiah, Jesus Christ, to bring the dwelling of our Holy God on earth in us. We are the tabernacles now not built by hand that our God dwells among as believers in Jesus Christ.

The placement of the furniture in the tabernacle is said to have been placed in the form of the cross, signifying the Cross Christ would bear for the world because of his great mercy and love to deliver us from our bondages of sins.

Old Tabernacle: Read the scriptures that are given for more detailed study of this subject. Exodus 25:8-9 Make me a sanctuary that I may dwell among them as I show you.

Exodus 31:1-11-Summary of work to be done
Exodus Chapter 40 discusses the order of the service of the Tabernacle (one gate, one door) Christ became our one door, one entry, one gate into the Presence of our Holy God and Father.

2 Chronicles Chapters (3-6) ; Solomon rebuilds the tabernacle chapter 4:22 entry of the house

Let's look at a few things of the Old Tabernacle and how each point to the coming Jesus Christ.

Altar: A Place of Worship, Fellowship, Prayer, Power, Wisdom and Dedication of offerings. It represented the place where one would die to self, to be raised to new life. Shows a place of complete surrender and repentance to God. We are to die daily to self that we may live according to our Holy Spirit. It was holy and nothing unclean could touch it or they would die.

Before one entered into the presence of God, because they were unworthy because of their sins, they had to bring sacrificial burnt offerings and other offerings that signified their complete dedication to God in all things to the altar..

Christ has come to the altar, being made the final sacrifice to make us worthy forever before God.

Ark of the Covenant: A box or chest that contained the 2 tablets of Testimony-which were the Ten Commandments and the Books of the Law. The ark represented the presence, power, goodness, the law or standard of holiness and faithfulness of God to his people.

Christ became the forever abiding presence, power, and wisdom of God. He came to not abolish the law, but he came to fulfill all the law.

Things placed in the ark:

1. The tablets of testimony (2 tablets-which were the Ten Commandments-10 commandments) Exodus 31:18 represented the law placed within.
   Christ by his Spirit has placed the Law within us.
2. Books of the Law –The 5 books written by Moses. (Genesis, Exodus, Leviticus, Numbers, and Deuteronomy)

Ark had a lid : Represents the seal of God over one's life.
Read Exodus 25 and 26 and 27 and Ephesians 4:3
The Holy Spirit is God's seal for eternity over our lives today after placing his laws and commandments in our heart by the Holy Spirit

Mercy Seat-Represents the mercy of God. God' grace and mercy by Christ Jesus is why we are here. His mercy covers us.

Manna-Food used to feed the children of Israel in the wilderness, to remind them of the provision of God. Christ became the way for which our God shall supply all our needs, especially our need to be freed from the bondage of sin and receive salvation and eternal life. He is our bread of life. He is our daily provider for all our provisions.

Cherubims-Angels represented his protection, his watchful eyes over his people and their ways. Angels were God's ministers to his people to keep and protect us in our all ways, to strengthen us as they did Jesus when he was tempted by Satan. Angels were known for their worship before the throne and to God, representing worship and fellowship with God.

Cherubim-Angels Exodus 23:20 Behold I send an Angel before thee, to keep thee in the way, and to bring thee into the place which I have prepared.

Cherubim-Angels Matthew 26:53 Thinkest thou that I cannot now pray to my Father, and he shall presently give me more than twelve legions of angels?

★★Jesus became greater than the angels, and is still sending the angels to minister to us.

Hebrews 1:4 Being made so much better than the angels, as he hath by inheritance obtained a more excellent name than they.

Aarons Staff- As a reminder to the rebels Numbers 17:10 God had chosen Aaron and his sons to be his High Priests. He chose Christ as well, and he has also chosen us. We are of the Royal Priesthood, by Christ Jesus. We are heirs to God and Co-heirs with Christ, who is our High priest. As believers in Jesus, we are children of God, the most high King.

Veil-Curtains that represented a separation or barrier of us from God because of our sins. Christ has come and torn down the veil -Hebrews 10:19-22 and Revelation 3:20. Jesus broken body was for us to have fellowship with God. We now can enter boldly at the throne of grace.

Colors .Exodus 26: 1 and 3, and 34 White curtains meant pure without sin, or stain or blemish. Blue curtains represents he which came from heaven, and the spiritual blessings provided to God's people in heaven. Purple curtains represented royalty, kingdom, and kingship. Red-scarlet curtains represented the color of the stain of our sin, and also the color of the blood that would cleanse us from all sins forever. Gold -represented the divine character of God.

Holiest of holies-Represent the dwelling place of God. Holy place of God's presence and dwelling.

One entry door/one entry gate Christ became our one way to enter into the Holy of Holies. He became the door for us to enter in for salvation and eternal life in the presence of God.

Outer Courts: The place where the sacrifices were offered-By Christ we no longer have to remain in the outer courts, we can come right into the inner courts.

Inner Courts: The place of worship before God.

Sacrificial lambs-Christ was the sacrifice-final sacrifice, he was sacrificed for our sins, no more animal sacrifices were needed. We must present ourselves as living sacrifices unto God.

Blood of animals –Signified cleansing from sins for the Priests and the Israelites. We are cleansed by the Blood of Jesus.

Olive oil Exodus 27:1, 20 21- Represented the anointing, healing, cleansing, and Light of God
Christ has become the light of the World shining the light of his love, salvation and eternal life on all he calls and all who receives his call. He became the anointed one with cleansing and healing in his body and blood.

Drink offering-Pouring of wine over the sacrifice caused a sweet aroma unto the Lord, showing God is pleased with the sacrifice.

Blood of Jesus is the wine poured out for the drink offering causing a sweet aroma over the sacrifice of his own body for a sinful world, as it pleased God to pour him out to save us from our sinful state, and became a sweet aroma as well to our God as we the believer carry the sweet aroma of Jesus Christ dwelling in us through the Holy Spirit.

Burning of incense and Sweet aroma spices unto the Lord-Again to cause a sweet aroma in the presence of God. Showing God is pleased with his people. Christ was the Son of God in whom God was well pleased.As we believe in Christ we become a sweet aroma that is well pleasing to God as Christ is.

Ransom money Exodus 36:11-16 The children of Israel paid ransom money for their sons to be bought back from bondage .

Christ Ransomed us. He set us free from sin. He brought us out of the bondage of sin in which we were prisoners to.

Redeemed – Redemption money
Bought back for a price. Ownership regained. A price had to be paid for that animal or thing to be given back to the owner. We have regained our freedom. Our rightful owner, God has regained us back from the Enemy-Satan. We have been redeemed by Christ.

Candlestick-Light of the temple. The lamps continually burned. Christ became the light of the world, forever. Lamps had branches coming from it, which represented Christ as the Branch or True Vine and we were the branches also to be grafted in, to be connected to this branch to be lights to the world, to shine bright in darkness, that the world will receive Jesus as Lord and Saviour.
John 8:12 ; John 12:46–source of light of the world.

Horns-signified power of God-Christ is now the power of God-he has been given all power and authority and has given us all power

Unleaven shewbread- The shewbread for the priests-was noted as the bread of life. It was without yeast, unleavened. Unleavened showbread represented –the bread of life without sin. Christ was perfect-without sin. No blemish was found in him. He became the bread that when we would partake of it, we would not hunger any more. He was our bread from heaven. Eating before God, represented fellowship with God. As we believed in the Son of God, Jesus, the bread of life, we come into fellowship with holy God.

Laver- A bowl used to hold the water for the various washings, to be done by the priests. Christ washed us by his blood and Holy Spirit. Ephesians 5:25-27.

The High Priests were (Aaron and his Sons) and The Levites (represented the 1ˢᵗ born males of the Israelites)

Priests**: Exodus Chapter 28 discusses the selection of Aaron and his sons only to serve as High priest. As well as Numbers 3:10-**And thou shalt appoint Aaron and his sons, and they shall wait on their priest's office: and the stranger that cometh nigh shall be put to death.

** Christ is our High Priest today.

Levite: They were the assistants to the priests. They were set aside by God to represent the 1ˢᵗ born of Israel.

** The Holy Spirit is our Helper/Assistant sent from God to all who believe in Christ.
Exodus 32:19 We see all the first born males of man and beast were to be set aside for the Lord.

Exodus 32:26 We see the Levites stand with Moses for the Lord.

Numbers Chapter 3 We see the Levites chosen by God to represent the 1ˢᵗ born males. And I, behold, I have taken the Levites from among the children of Israel instead of all the firstborn that openeth the matrix among the children of Israel: therefore the Levites shall be mine; Because all the firstborn *are* mine; *for* on the day that I smote all the firstborn in the land of Egypt I hallowed unto me all the firstborn in Israel, both man and beast: mine shall they be: I *am* the LORD.

The Levites were the ones to whom the tithes were to now be assigned or given to for the work they performed daily in the temple. The people were to bring the tithe unto the Lord and it would be assigned -specifically for the Levite, and the Levite would tithe unto the Lord, off the tithe given to him, as his inheritance for the Lord. The other Offerings that were brought by the children of Israel were presented to the High Priest for their inheritance and for the atonement/cleansing of sins for the Israelites, as well to be used for the Israelite individual or family in response to thanksgiving and worship before the Lord. The tithe would be eaten before the Lord in worship.

The tithe was usually not in money format. Although money was given, such as atonement money, and redemption money, but the tithe was always in produce of the land and animals.
The tithe was turned into money only if the destination they had to travel to was a long distance and it was not feasible to carry the sacrifices for such a distance. At this time, they were permitted to take money to the destination and once they arrived they were to purchase the required animals and grains that were to be given to the Lord.

This is why the offerings were spoken as two in Malachi chapter 3, as Tithe and offerings, because though they were both offerings, their purpose were different. Tithe given to the Levite was set aside as holy unto the Lord as the Levite was, separate and different. This is why it is stated in Malachi-You rob me in Tithe and offerings. This meant The Israelites were not bringing not only their offerings for cleansing of their sins but they were not even bringing the Priests and the Levite their required offerings -the tithe as commanded by God.

In Numbers Chapters 16-18 We also, see a rebellion of a particular clan of the Levites against Moses and Aarons and his Sons, the High Priests, that God deals with emphatically and then re-emphasizes to the Levites that they were not chosen to be High Priest. They were set aside for another purpose as priests of God and they should not take it upon themselves again to be disobedient to him in rebelling against his chosen High Priests.

Who is the high Priest today? Christ

Are there still Levites? NO, because there is no more a Levitical priesthood. Christ is the Great High Priest-who replaced Aaron and his Sons, and the Levites. He did it alone on the cross. Christ is the only mediator needed now. He is the only way to the Father. None can go to the Father except by Christ.

Christ is reaching the world through every believer as we apply his word in our lives in every situation of life, just as we saw Jesus Christ did, so that others may see him through us and our living. See his love, obedience, perserverance, faith, endurance, strength, grace, mercy, suffering, humility to the will of the Father, no matter the situations, and so on and so forth. All that the father may be glorified and his character, and power manifested for us, and for others around us. This is so we may grow in a stronger trust in God and that others too will put their trust in God and glorify him. That others too may be Saved. God is still about his business of reconciling a world back to himself. He uses us to work this plan daily.
God is in all things always. We must remember this and live according to this word. His word spoken to us.

The Levite was not needed for Christ's Priesthood. Christ did not come from the Levitical tribe but from the Tribe of Judah, a tribe where no priest had ever come from.

Read Hebrew 7:11-22

What has happened to the Levite? They are no more. They were part of the Old Tabernacle set up. So since there are no more Levites, there is no need for the tithe to be taken to the Levite, therefore there is no more tithing required because the Law has changed. The covenant has changed. The old tabernacle ordinances are no longer required by the letter. They are fulfilled by the Spirit in this new tabernacle.

***Also, the Levites were assistants to the High Priest. Today Christ our High Priest does have an assistant. His name is Holy Spirit. Our helper/assistant/comforter. The Holy Spirit is the assistant in the temple that he dwells, which is our body. Our body is the temple of our Holy God and his Son, Our high priest, and the helper/assistant the Holy Spirit.

What happened to the Offerings? Christ became the final offering. However, we are required to set aside at the beginning of every week an amount to give for the service of the tabernacle and it's works in the community and for the blessing of the saints, poor, widows, workers,etc.

Are there still sacrifices and offerings -as were made in the Old Tabernacle? NO, but Giving is still required in the New Covenant and the New Tabernacle. We are the tabernacles/temples of God where he has set his Name and his spirit, however, we still are to give money to our churches, the physical structure given for the assembly of God's people, as God stirs our heart to give. We are still to assemble at the place of God, forsaking not the assembly of ourselves as commanded by God. We are still to offer ourselves as living sacrifices to our God daily. We are still to give the offering of thanksgiving and praise with our lips.

Do you see that the Old Tabernacle was foreshadowing the tabernacle that would come later when Christ the Messiah came.

There were different types of offerings/ordinances/festivals that were to be kept under the Old Covenant for the Old Tabernacle.

Exodus 12:14 And this day shall be unto you for a memorial; and ye shall keep it a feast to the LORD throughout your generations; ye shall keep it a feast **by an ordinance for ever.**

Thank God that he has sent Christ and fulfilled them forever.

Various Offerings, and many Holy Convocations/Celebrations/ Days, as well as all the other ordinances for the Old Tabernacle were given by God to the children of Israel through Abraham and Moses

There were many things required by the children of Israel to be observed as remembrance of their covenant and deliverance from Egypt. These things were to be done only- until CHRIST came- until Grace came and fulfilled Law. After he came we would no longer be under the schoolmaster –The Law.

Read:

Galatians 3:25 But after that faith is come, we are no longer under a schoolmaster.

Hebrews 9:1, 10 Then verily the first *covenant* had also ordinances of divine service, and a worldly sanctuary. *Which stood* only in meats and drinks, and divers washings, and carnal ordinances, imposed *on them* until the time of reformation.

Ephesian 2:15 Having abolished in his flesh the enmity, *even* the law of commandments *contained* in ordinances; for to make in himself of twain one new man, *so* making peace;

Colossians 2:20-21 Wherefore if ye be dead with Christ from the rudiments of the world, why, as though living in the world, are ye subject to ordinances,
(Touch not; taste not; handle not;)

This was in regards to all the rules and regulations that are found in Genesis through Deuteronomy of how they could not eat this meat, don't touch a dead body, don't touch a woman with a blood issue, don't touch a leper, etc. and so forth. Reading the laws of then would make your head spin, and the worse, many of the violations meant death, even if you did not observe certain festivals, death. This was used by God to show his people that sin is truly death and not life. Thanks be to God for Christ, who has delivered us from Sin forever and has given us Abundant and Eternal life.

Offerings:

Offerings that were made unto the Lord, were to be set apart as holy, consecrated offerings unto the Lord. Offerings given by the people shows a people humbling, setting themselves apart before God. Offering themselves unto him for service. Christ would come later to demonstrate the final offering. The Offering of himself as set apart by God to atone for the sins of the people, to redeem them back from their sinful state. We now must present ourselves as living sacrifices unto the Lord and we too will become the sweet savour/ aroma to God as we are in Christ.

Read:

2 Corinthians 2:15 For we are unto God a sweet savour (aroma) of Christ, in them that are saved, and in them that perish:

Let's discuss some of these offerings and festivals that Christ has also fulfilled

Leviticus 22:17-31 Talks about how the offerings were to be without blemish. Christ was without blemish. Christ in us is our righteousness before God. As Christ is in us, he makes us without blemish before the Father when we come before the Father. This is why we can come boldly to the throne of grace that we might find his mercy. It is because we are hid in Christ. It is because of Christ we can bring all of our good and wrong to the Father and find forgiveness, love, kindness, grace and mercy, and new compassions daily.

Leviticus 7:11-16 Heave offering was part of the peace offering. Which could be thanksgiving offering, vow offering, fellowship offering, or free will offering.

Tithe: The tithe was actually instituted before the Mosaic Laws as we see Abraham paying a tenth to the Most High priest Melchizedec, which we will learn was an allegory of things to come

It then became the tenth of all increase from the land and animals given to the priests as holy and devoted thing to God in worship and thanksgiving unto God, showing fear unto the Lord for his blessings, deliverance, and victory.

God would later tell Moses to assign the tithe to be specifically for the Levites, who God would choose for the service of the tabernacle as assistants to the High Priest.

Read the Following:
Leviticus 27:30-34 and Deuteronomy 12:1-14- discusses Tithe offering by the Israelties

Genesis 14:18-20 Abraham meets Melchizedek and gives him a tithe of all the spoil/fruit/increase from the battle

Numbers 18:21-32; Deuteronomy 14:22-29; Deuteronomy 26:12-19 Nehemiah 10:35-39

2 Chronicles Chapter 31 – discusses all the portion and tithe assigned to the priests and the Levites: -

2 Chronicles 31:4-6 Moreover he commanded the people that dwelt in Jerusalem to give the portion of the priests and the Levites, that they might be encouraged in the law of the LORD. And as soon as the commandment came abroad, the children of Israel brought in abundance the firstfruits of corn, wine, and oil, and honey, and of all the increase of the field; and the tithe of all *things* brought they in abundantly. And *concerning* the children of Israel and Judah, that dwelt in the cities of Judah, they also brought in the tithe of oxen and sheep, and the tithe of holy things which were consecrated unto the LORD their God, and laid *them* by heaps.

The Levites purpose -Numbers chapters 3 and Chapter 4

Offerings of 1ˢᵗ born of man and animal Exodus 13:1-2 And the LORD spake unto Moses, saying, Sanctify unto me all the firstborn, whatsoever openeth the womb among the children of Israel, *both* of man and of beast: it *is* mine

Exodus 34: 19 All that openeth the matrix *is* mine; and every firstling among thy cattle, *whether* ox or sheep, *that is male.*

Offerings Cleansing from issue of blood -Leviticus 12:7 to be cleansed from issue of blood

In Mark 5:25-34 Jesus came and healed the woman who had the issue of blood for 12 years. In Matthew 8:2-4 He healed the leper and told him to go show himself to the priest as a testimony to them that there was one in the midst greater, with power to forgive sins and heal showing fulfillment, without an animal sacrifice being taken to the priest first.

First Fruits

With First Fruits the Israelites were honoring God in thanking him for choosing them as his people, his first fruits. As being their God and they his chosen people.

It expressed to him thanksgiving, for his calling and chosing them as his people to be their God. To do in remembrance for his giving the land that they were on their way to as they left the land of Egypt, a place of bondage and bitterness, to a land flowing with milk and honey. They understood all that they had were from the blessing of God and all that they would receive later would also be through his blessings as well. They understood that everything belonged to God. They started giving to him as he commanded them, even before they came into the land of milk and honey. He wanted them to reverence him as their provider always. With the small as well as with what they would receive once they arrived in the promised land. He used firstfruits as a way to remind the people to always put him first in their lives.

Exodus 34:26 The first of the firstfruits of thy land thou shalt bring unto the house of the LORD thy God. Thou shalt not seethe a kid in his mother's milk.

Exodus 34:22 And thou shalt observe the feast of weeks, of the firstfruits of wheat harvest, and the feast of ingathering at the year's end.

Our high priest no longer requires the tithe and first fruits as were required to be given to the Levite and by the Israelites for their own families. Christ became the first fruit, depositing in all who believe in him, the 1st fruit of his Holy Spirit, making us 1st fruits.

Read the following scriptures:

1 Corinthians 15:20-23 But now is **Christ risen from the dead, _and_ become the firstfruits** of them that slept. For since by man _came_ death, by man _came_ also the resurrection of the dead. For as in

Adam all die, even so in Christ shall all be made alive. But each in his own order: Christ the first fruits, after that those who are Christ's at His coming,

The Holy Spirit is First fruits: Read the following.

First fruits of the Spirit: Romans 8:23 And not only *they*, but ourselves also, **which have the firstfruits of the Spirit**, even we ourselves groan within ourselves, waiting for the adoption, *to wit*, the redemption of our body.
We have the first fruits- of the Spirit-as believers.--(bringing of first fruits is the Christian-the Believer in Christ in whom dwells the Holy Spirit-as we come into his presence as a believer we bring the Holy Spirit and its fruit.)

James 1:18 shows that we as believers in Christ are first fruits

1 Corinthians 16:15 I beseech you, brethren, (ye know the house of Stephanas, that it is the firstfruits of Achaia, and *that* they have addicted themselves to the ministry of the saints,)

The house of Stephanas were the new converts believers in Christ. They had believed on him making them first fruits in that area.

This is why **Romans 12:1** Says present your selves a living sacrifice, holy and acceptable unto God.

So that we might become First fruits also.

★★★Teaching bringing the tithe (10%), first fruits, and offerings is not wrong teaching or theology.

What we have to understand is that bringing the tithe today since Christ has come and fulfilled the law is different than it was in the Old Tabernacle of the Israelite days. It was to be brought by the letter back then, now it is brought in the Spirit dwelling in your heart as believers in Christ.

Now it is brought fulfilled as the Holy Spirit in us. So everytime a believer walks in the doors of the church, the Holy Spirit in them, they have-the tithe and offering fulfilled in the body-by Christ Jesus- Glory to God. This is a blessing. Yes, as believers are the walking, breathing, talking, powerful- tithe and offering, and God will bless us as he promised every time we come to the house of worship and everyday where ever we are. Also we are the house of worship, the temple of God as well . He will open the windows of heaven and pour you out a blessing you will not have room to receive. However, forsake not the assembling of yourselves in the house of God as believers. Trust in Jesus today. There is a shower of blessing waiting there for you each and every time. He will bless your going out and coming in wherever you go.

So you can still clap, stand, and say amen when the preacher is teaching the law of tithe and offering, because you understand what he is teaching is truth. Yes tithe and offering should be brought to the house of God, and yes you will receive blessing. However, you understand that Jesus is the tithe and offering FULFILLED by dwelling in you by his Spirit, and you are not under the old method according to the law-by the letter, you are under the new method according to Grace- by the Spirit, which is like Chicken Campbell Soup. MMMM good.

Now, Listen and listen good:

Giving money is still required to be done to the church. It takes money to feed the homeless, take care of the poor, widows, orphans, and church members in need, to do mission work, send the gospel around the world, to give to local charities, schools and organizations in your community, to keep the lights on in the church, to pay the pastors, and other workers of the church, etc and so forth.

Giving is still required. He says set aside weekly for the saints, he says give and it shall be given, but he does not stipulate a particular percentage. Give according as he has prospered you, and according to your ability given by God. Don't let man condemn you any longer if it is not 10%.

God has removed that curse of the law by fulfilling it.

Did you catch that. The way God removed the curse of the Law was through the crucifixion of Christ on the cross where the law and sin were nailed, thereby fulfilling the law and removing the curse of the law by Christ forever.

Galatians 3:13 Christ hath redeemed us from the curse of the law, being made a curse for us: for it is written, Cursed *is* every one that hangeth on a tree:

Colossians 2:14 Blotting out the handwriting of ordinances that was against us, which was contrary to us, and took it out of the way, nailing it to his cross;

Grain/Burnt/Fellowship offerings/Trespass/Guilt offering/ Purification and Peace offerings:

Ezekiel 45:13-16 offerings in these verses were wheat, barley, and sheep that were used to make atonement for the people of Israel. Atonement offering means act of reconciling one back from their sinful state into their rightful place with God. If they had committed any type of sin, if they had touched anything unclean, stole, killed, lied, not kept a vow, etc. and so forth, these offering were to be taken to the priest so they might be cleansed and forgiven from their sins, and reconciled back to God. Christ was the last offering

Leviticus Chapter 2 –Talks about the grain offering to be prepared with Olive oil, and no yeast.

And the Drink offering-to be poured over the meat and grain offering, making a sweet aroma to God

The Olive oil represented the Anointing and the Light of the Lamps of the tabernacle that would burn continually as stated in **Leviticus 24:1-2**

Today we know we who have believed on Christ, The Anointed, have too been anointed with his Holy Spirit and adopted into the family of God, and are co-heirs/joint heirs with Christ in all things. We know he is the light of the world and as he dwell in us, we should be reflections of his Light, that should burn continually in and through each believer forever.

Luke 4:16-21 This is where Jesus states his anointing.

John 8:12 Then spake Jesus again unto them, saying, I am the light of the world: he that followeth me shall not walk in darkness, but shall have the light of life.

2 Corinthians 2:14-15 But thanks be to God, who always leads us as captives in Christ's triumphal procession and uses us to spread the aroma of the knowledge of him everywhere. For we are to God the pleasing aroma of Christ among those who are being saved and those who are perishing

He was poured out as the drink offering for our sins to make us a sweet aroma

Ephesians 5:2 And walk in love, as Christ also hath loved us, and hath given himself for us an offering and a sacrifice to God for a sweet smelling savour.

Leviticus Chapter 1 Talks about the burnt offering- Burnt offering- shows total dedication of ourselves to God just as Christ became totally surrendered to the Father to dedicate his life for us. This was the complete annihilation of self to God. Complete surrender of self to God and his works in his ways for his will and purposes.

Leviticus Chapter 3 –Talks about the Fellowship offering. observance that the Israelites now had this amazing fellowship with God, and were to serve no other god, for he was their God and they were his people

Leviticus Chapters 4 and 5 Talks about Trespass/Guilt offering/ and begins to speak on how the Levites are to prepare the burnt, grain, fellowship and sin offerings.We have been forgiven of all trespasses and sin. Freed from all guilt and shame by faith in Jesus.

Leviticus 12:6 Purification offerings- after birth of a child, and any issue of blood.
Our purity is only by a Pure Jesus.

Exodus 24:5 Peace offerings And he sent young men of the children of Israel, which offered burnt offerings, and sacrificed peace offerings of oxen unto the LORD. Jesus is our Lord. He is our Peace.

Leviticus 11 Discusses the clean and unclean food they could not eat.

Atonement for sins

Atonement definition: (by Free dictionary) Satisfaction for an injury or wrong.

Exodus 32:30 And it came to pass on the morrow, that Moses said unto the people, Ye have sinned a great sin: and now I will go up unto the LORD; peradventure I shall make an atonement for your sin.

Atonement blood:
Leviticus 17:11 For the life of the flesh *is* in the blood: and I have given it to you upon the altar to make an atonement for your souls: for it *is* the blood *that* maketh an atonement for the soul.

Atonement money:

Exodus 30:12-16 When thou takest the sum of the children of Israel after their number, then shall they give every man a ransom for his soul unto the LORD, when thou numberest them; that there be no plague among them, when *thou* numberest them. This they shall give, every one that passeth among them that are numbered, half a shekel after the shekel of the sanctuary: (a shekel *is* twenty gerahs:) an half shekel *shall be* the offering of the LORD. Every one that passeth among them that are numbered, from twenty years old and above, shall give an offering unto the LORD. The rich shall not give more, and the poor shall not give less than half a shekel, when *they* give an offering unto the LORD, to make an atonement for your souls. And thou shalt take the atonement money of the children of Israel, and shalt appoint it for the service of the tabernacle of the congregation; that it may be a memorial unto the children of Israel before the LORD, to make an atonement for your souls.

Who pays atonement money in the church today. Anyone preaching sermons on atonement money like they preach on the Tithe. NO. Why? Because Christ paid the price for the World's Atonement. So why is it we can believe he paid the price for our atonement and that there is no need for atonement money to be paid or fulfilled by us, why can't we believe the same about the Tithe. Why can't we believe it too has been paid, fulfilled by Christ.

Redemption money-being bought back —redeemed after being sold into slavery to serve another.

Leviticus 25:50 And he shall reckon with him that bought him from the year that he was sold to him unto the year of jubile: and the price of his sale shall be according unto the number of years, according to the time of an hired servant shall it be with him. If *there be* yet many years *behind*, according unto them he shall give again the price of his redemption out of the money that he was bought for. And if there remain but few years unto the year of jubile, then he shall count with him, *and* according unto his years shall he give him again the price of his redemption.

Isaiah 52:3 For thus saith the LORD, Ye have sold yourselves for nought; and ye shall be redeemed without money.

★★ be redeemed without money- God has redeemed us without money. He has redeemed us with blood. By the blood and body of his Son Jesus Christ.

Prophecy of the coming Christ to come to redeem us without money

Isaiah 55:1 Ho, every one that thirsteth, come ye to the waters, and he that hath no money; come ye, buy, and eat; yea, come, buy wine and milk without money and without price.

Money to be devoted to God as holy:

Corban: some have thought this to be the tithe in money format- since it too was money to be devoted to God —but Christ tells the Pharisees it was unlawful for them to tell the people they could not use it to honor their mother and Father. (This sounds like the teaching today in many churches today concerning tithe and offerings–that if any portion of the tithe is used to take care of their family, parents, etc. they would be cursed for it was to be devoted wholly to God. Not recognizing Christ was the Fulfillment of this type offering, and not even recognizing that even in the law it states if you did not honor your Father and Mother you could be put to death.)

Mark 7:10- 11 For Moses said, Honour thy father and thy mother; and, Whoso curseth father or mother, let him die the death, But ye say,

If a man shall say to his father or mother, *It is* Corban, that is to say, a gift, by whatsoever thou mightest be profited by me; *he shall be free.*

They and some today still are condemning the guiltless, saying it is wrong to help others or your own family by paying a bill to take care of your family. This is why Jesus corrected the religious sector with the following scripture.

Matthew 12:7 But if ye had known what this meaneth, I will have mercy, and not sacrifice, ye would not have condemned the guiltless.

*** Christ has paid the price for us, his blood has redeemed us and atoned for all our sins. Glory to God for his Grace and Mercy. Christ is our Redeemer, our Redeemer lives.

1 Corinthians 6:20 For ye are bought with a price: therefore glorify God in your body, and in your spirit, which are God's.

Colossians 1:14 In whom we have redemption through his blood, *even* the forgiveness of sins:

Various washings/cleansings/purification process:

Exodus 30:17-21 Talks about the various washings to be done by the priests
We now are a royal priesthood washed in the blood of our Lord and Saviour Jesus Christ, cleansed forever.

Some of the festivals Holy convocations–celebrations/ memorials that were to be observed:Celebrations to honor God for the goodness, peace, and rest of God in their lives.

Leviticus Chapter 23 talks about All the various feasts/celebrations/ festivals that the Lord instituted to be observed by the children of Israel forever in every generation. In all these festivals they would rest, then bring the various offerings as discussed above.

Solemn festival usually referred to the Passover, Feast of Weeks and Feast of Tabernacles

Deut 16:15 Seven days shalt thou keep a solemn feast unto the LORD thy God in the place which the LORD shall choose: because the LORD thy God shall bless thee in all thine increase, and in all the works of thine hands, therefore thou shalt surely rejoice

Sabbath- Exodus 31:13 Speak thou also unto the children of Israel, saying, Verily my sabbaths ye shall keep: for it *is* a sign between me and you throughout your generations; that *ye* may know that I *am* the LORD that doth sanctify you.
An observance of the day God delivered the Israelites, his people, from their hard labors in Egypt, and taking them to a land flowing with milk and honey.
A rest to his people. Today Christ says for us to come to him and find rest. Yes, we should also take time to rest our bodies, but there is a greater rest he wants us to enter into because he has prepared it for us by his body and blood. **Read Matthew 11:28-30**

Exodus 12:1-43 Passover- To celebrate the Day the Lord spared their lives by passing over the homes that had the blood of the sacrifice on the lintel and sides of the door posts. All homes who had the blood were saved. (Only the blood of a first year/ 1 year old male lamb could be used) Jesus Christ has caused our lives to be spared from wrath and condemnation and eternal hell.

Also read Exodus 13:1-16

Christ met the requirement of becoming the sacrificial lamb of our Passover, as he was the 1st male child born to the virgin Mary and Joseph, whose blood was sacrificed that our lives might be saved.

Leviticus 23:10-17 Festival of leavened bread-Now they could eat bread with yeast as they were now in the land of plenty and now reconciled back to God. No longer in a place of contamination of sin and bondage. Let us celebrate our deliverance from our sin

nature through Christ as he dwells in each believer. We have been reconciled back to God through faith in Jesus.
We are no longer in our place of bondage.

Memorial of Trumpet Blasts/Blowing of the Trumpets-a solemn feast: Numbers 10:1-10

Sound your Trumpet. Let us also make a joyful noise with our lips for all he has done, is doing and will forever do for his children.

Festival of Tabernacles: Deut 16:16-17 Three times in a year shall all thy males appear before the LORD thy God in the place which he shall choose; in the feast of unleavened bread, and in the feast of weeks, and in the feast of tabernacles: and they shall not appear before the LORD empty Every man *shall give* as he is able, according to the blessing of the LORD thy God which he hath given thee.

Deuteronomy 16:13-14 Thou shalt observe the feast of tabernacles seven days, after that thou hast gathered in thy corn and thy wine And thou shalt rejoice in thy feast, thou, and thy son, and thy daughter, and thy manservant, and thy maidservant, and the Levite, the stranger, and the fatherless, and the widow, that *are* within thy gates.

Let us celebrate the goodness of God. Let us bless his name at all times, and worship him with faithfulness all the days of our life on earth.

Feast of Unleavened bread, Feast of Harvest, Feast of ingathering

Exodus 34:18 —Observance of when God brought them out of Egypt that midnight. They could not eat bread with yeast, thereby it was unleavened, they were leaving the affliction behind them.

Do you remember midnight situations, God has brought you out. If you are in a midnight now, trust God he will bring you out. Midnight does not last forever.

Exodus 23:14-16 Three times thou shalt keep a feast unto me in the year: **Feast of Unleavened bread; Feast of harvest-1st fruits** that were to be brought with the early crops and **Feast of ingathering** which were to brought with the crops that came in towards end of year.

Let us gather for worship to our God.

v.17 It is at these 3 times per year, at the above 3 festivals, that all the males must appear before the Lord

Deut 16:3 Thou shalt eat no leavened bread with it; seven days shalt thou eat unleavened bread therewith, *even* the bread of affliction; for thou camest forth out of the land of Egypt in haste: that thou mayest remember the day when thou camest forth out of the land of Egypt all the days of thy life.

Celebrate as we remember the goodness of our God.

The feast of weeks- after 7 complete Sabbaths. The day after as the 1st day through 50 days, then offer a new meat and grain offering in the form of 2 baked loaves with leaven –they are the firstfruits unto the Lord. 7 lambs without blemish of 1st year, 1 bull/cattle, 2 rams. Drink offering of wine

Feast of weeks- also known as feast of harvests and day of 1st fruits, and Pentecost. They were not to eat any of the harvest before bringing the first fruits to God. Acknowledging we are putting God 1st.

Christ then came being the kingdom, this is why we are to seek ye first the kingdom of God. This is putting God 1st in our lives above all things when we seek to receive Christ the first as first in and over our lives, making us first fruits as well, as his Holy Spirit dwells in us.

Feast of weeks Lasted only 1 day. Eating of leaven bread instead of unleaven bread meant they praised God for his daily provisions for his people, and thanks giving for the opportunity to be in fellowship with him in every aspect of our lives.

Feast of the dedication -John 10:22 And it was at Jerusalem the feast of the dedication, and it was winter.

Let us dedicate our lives to our Holy God.

Festival of Booths: Leviticus 23:41-43 and Nehemiah 8:14-18

New Moon festival –Observed because it was it was midnight when they were delivered from Egypt. 1 Chronicles 23:29-31-Nehemiah 10:32-33

Read the following scriptures to show the fulfillment in Christ of all these offerings and festivals.

Galatians Chapter 5- Stand fast in the Grace of God

Galatians 6:6-18 Christ finished it all

Colossians Chapter 2 Christ finished it all

Hebrews Chapter 10 Christ finished it all

Do you now understand now, how God set the Old Tabernacle and Old Covenant up as a foreshadow of Jesus, our Messiah. There are so many more things that could be discussed from the silver rings, the badger skins, the specific measurement, but time does not allow. However, every detail given by God to Moses to build the tabernacle, was a foreshadow of Christ's coming to fulfill the things of the Old Tabernacle.

Christ became our Sabbath, and all the Festivals. He became our rest and reason to celebrate the goodness of God. Christ became the price paid for our redemption and atonement for our sins. He became our reconciliation back to God for our liberty/freedom. He whom the Son sets free is free indeed. This is why we must standfast in our liberty, and do not be entangled in bondage again. The price he paid was too great. He was our deliverance, salvation, purification, sanctification, consecration-making us holy before God forever. He became our restoration and reconciliation to our Holy God. He tore down the barriers, the veils. He removed the outer and inner courts that we can come boldly into the Holy of Holies. He made us his holy temple where he abides forever by the Holy Spirit. JESUS IS LORD. We now can worship him in SPIRIT and in TRUTH – FOREVER. The ordinances have been kept forever. For the Lord does not change. He has kept all his law and ordinances by CHRIST-one man, and one final offering. He was our Pass Over lamb. He was the first of many brethren. He was the best of the best. His blood has washed us, cleansed, and purified us forever. We celebrate him, as we receive him as Lord and Saviour in our lives and his Holy Spirit comes and abides in us and we become ambassadors for Christ for others to see the light of Jesus in and through our holy lives and living, that they will come want to partake in this Bread of Life forever more.

Sacrifices and offerings Today

Hebrews 13:15-16 By him therefore let us offer the sacrifices of praise to God continually that is the fruit of our lips giving thanks to his name. But to do good and to communicate forget not. For with such sacrifices God is well pleased.

Romans 12:1-3 Present yourselves a living sacrifice.

Celebrating Christ Today, through various Holidays etc.:

Should we still celebrate Christ. Yes, just like we celebrate him through Christmas, Easter, Thanksgiving and so many other ways. If you want to continue to observe Passover, Sabbath Lent, Festival of Booths, Festival of Tabernacles, by all means do it. He is worthy of all celebrations. Just like we celebrate our other special days, like our

Anniversaries, Birthdays, 4th of July, Veterans Day, Martin Luther King Days, President Day, Etc.

They are still celebrations recognizing Christ or Someone else, done in remembrance. However, we are not obligated to celebrate them. We are no longer cursed and put to death if we do not celebrate them.

Christ, did institute THE COMMUNION for all believers to celebrate and remember him giving His Body and His Blood that was broken and shed for the atonement of our sins, for our redemption from bondage, for our purification, peace, sanctification, justification, consecration, salvation, and eternal life.

1 Corinthians 10:16-17

The cup of blessing which we bless, is it not the communion of the blood of Christ? The bread which we break, is it not the communion of the body of Christ? For we *being* many are one bread, *and* one body: for we are all partakers of that one bread.

1 Corinthians 11:23-30

For I have received of the Lord that which also I delivered unto you, That the Lord Jesus the *same* night in which he was betrayed took bread: And when he had given thanks, he brake *it*, and said, Take, eat: this is my body, which is broken for you: this do in remembrance of me. After the same manner also *he took* the cup, when he had supped, saying, This cup is the new testament in my blood: this do ye, as oft as ye drink *it*, in remembrance of me For as often as ye eat this bread, and drink this cup, ye do shew the Lord's death till he come. Wherefore whosoever shall eat this bread, and drink *this* cup of the Lord, unworthily, shall be guilty of the body and blood of the Lord. But let a man examine himself, and so let him eat of *that* bread, and drink of *that* cup. For he that eateth and drinketh unworthily, eateth and drinketh damnation to himself, not discerning the Lord's body. For this cause many *are* weak and sickly among you, and many sleep.

The following are just a few our our special days we celebrate in America. Is there anything wrong with celebrating them? No. Are we cursed if we don't? No

Our celebrations:

1. Birthdays
2. Anniversaries
3. Graduations
4. Memorial Day
5. Independence Day (Fourth of July)
6. Baby showers
7. Wedding Showers
8. Martin Luther King Day
9. President's Day
10. Veteran's day
11. Valentine's day
12. Columbus Day

There are many things that were done according to the Law as commanded by God to celebrate him etc. The following are a few things today we still do in remembrance to celebrate Christ.

1. Christmas
2. Easter
3. Passover
4. Sabbath
5. Feast of Unleavened bread
6. Festival of Moon
7. Harvest Festival
8. Ingathering Festival
9. Feast of Weeks
10. Feast of Tabernacles/Booths
11. Feast of New moons or Moon
12. Feast of Trumpets

13. Daniel Fast
14. Ash Wednesday
15. Lent

Is there anything wrong with any one Celebrating Christ in these ways, on these holidays? Is there anything wrong with honoring him in these things for WHO he is and WHAT he has done? No, God is pleased. But he does not require them either, be done by the letter as they were in biblical times. If you want to observe one of these celebrations or others unto God. That is fine. Do not however get in strife over one day over the other, and who is wrong or right if one celebrates one day and one does not. I do some of them. I do not do all of them, and neither do you. I don't feel condemned for not doing them. I don't feel cursed for not doing them. If I listened to some, I would feel condemned and cursed. I have chosen to listen to my heavenly Father. He says he is well pleased with me and any holiday or day I choose to celebrate him, even if I don't choose a day. For me to just daily give him the sacrifice of praise and thanksgiving daily from my lips, and serve him in my day to day living by walking In brotherly love and in obedience daily to his direction would be enough for him. However, he desires us celebrate him and his goodness. Let us celebrate and remember him. Let our kids enjoy these special events in life along with other children while using them as moments to teach them about Christ and that we should celebrate him and honor him. There is nothing wrong with Easter Egg Hunts in celebration of Christ, and an understanding of how just as we search for the hidden or lost egg and candy, Christ searched for us and found us and saw we were good. That is a good chuckle and spiritual kid lesson. There is nothing wrong with celebrating Christmas with trees, lights, gifts, laughter, fun, while teaching that Christ died on a cross (made from wood of a tree) that he might become the light of the world and the greatest gift to the world that we might have peace, and this laughter and fun today and might be saved from all our sins. A great reason to celebrate today and everyday about the goodness of Jesus, and how we honor our God with our celebrations. However, do not make the holidays a reason to curse or get into strife with one another over. It is not a sin to do it and not a sin to not keep such holidays. What is important that you choose your way to Celebrate and Honor our God and remember his Son.

This is what God addressed in **Romans Chapter 14**. Believers were getting in strife over days they chose to honor God and over the eating of meats or herbs. Stop getting in strife over this. If you want to celebrate Christ through Christmas, celebrate Him in that way. I am. If you don't, that is fine. You want to celebrate him through Easter, Good Friday, Festival of Moon, Daniel Fast, Ash Wednesday, Passover, Lent, etc. Do it.

Don't condemn one another over these things, as believers in Christ. God said they are all good. Some things may be Law, some may be according to Grace, but neither is a sin.
It's like 2 people arguing over whether a car is better if it is blue and the other said no it is better if it is Red, and God is shaking his head, saying really, neither is Sin. You will be no better off if you choose the Red over the Blue.

You are no better off if you Celebrate Christmas and Easter etc, and you are no worse off if you do not celebrate them, and vice versa. **What matters is that you are a Believer in Christ. You have received him as Lord and Saviour and celebrate him in some way even if it is just lifting your voice in praise to him.**

Do not frustrate the GRACE of God on your life by living legalistically.

1 Corinthians 8:8 But meat commendeth us not to God: for neither, if we eat, are we the better; neither, if we eat not, are we the worse.

The same as was with the debate over the meat here, is with the celebrations and observance of various days. God said give me thanks for all things and eat what you want.

1 Timothy 4:1,3-5 Now the Spirit speaketh expressly, that in the latter times some shall depart from the faith, giving heed to seducing spirit, and doctrines of devils; .. Forbidding to marry, and commanding to abstain from meats, which God hath created to be received with thanksgiving of them which believe and know the truth**. For every creature of God is good, and nothing to be refused, if it be received with thanksgiving: For it is sanctified by the word of God and prayer.**

Thank the Lord for your meal, Pray over your food and bon appetit. Eat what you like, and don't eat what you don't like. Always, Always do all things in moderation.

Now again we know that only if you are a stronger Christian in your walk can you receive the above and correct it. If you are still a bit weak in accepting this as the Pharisees were at the time and as we all have been and still are in many areas that is ok. Continue to do as you believe is pleasing to God in this season and he will be pleased with you as he continues to mold us on his Potter's wheel.

Revisit Romans 14:1-4 again.

Now, don't walk in pride, either. If you are thinking you have been a preacher, and a teacher, a believer, for so long, that God cannot show you new revelation in his word, when God said we will continue to be growing until we see him face to face, well remember, pride comes before the fall. He desires we humble ourselves as children under his mighty hand and be obedient to him, every time he shows us more of who he is and what he has provided. We don't have to force the word of TRUTH down anyone's throat. Remember he-GOD- is able to make his servant stand.

Remember as our revelation grows from God. We are to put away the way we thought as a child and walk in our more matured (renewed) Spirit, being more spiritually minded rather than carnally minded and walk in the newness of our spirits and mind which God is renewing daily.

We do realize by now he says there is an Old and a New Covenant and the Old Covenant is no more. Old covenant is fulfilled through Christ, who is the New Covenant.

God promised that he would establish a better and new covenant with his people. A covenant that would not be written in stone on tablets, but now on the hearts of his people, because he was sending the Holy Spirit to be in our hearts.

Read the following:

The covenant written on tablets:

Exodus 34:1 And the Lord said unto Moses, Hew two tables of stone like unto the first: and I will write upon these tables the words that were in the first tables, which thou brakest.
v. 27 – 28 And the Lord said unto Moses, Write thou these words: for after the tenor of these words, I have made a covenant with thee and with Israel. And he was there with the Lord forty days and forty nights; he did neither eat bread, nor drink water. And he wrote upon the tables the words of the covenant, the ten commandments.

The promise of the covenant to be written on hearts.

Jeremiah 31:31-33 Behold, the days come, saith the LORD, that I will make a new covenant with the house of Israel, and with the house of Judah Not according to the covenant that I made with their fathers in the day *that* I took them by the hand to bring them out of the land of Egypt; which my covenant they brake, although I was an husband unto them, saith the LORD: But this *shall be* the covenant that I will make with the house of Israel; After those days, saith the LORD, I will put my law in their inward parts, and write it in their hearts; and will be their God, and they shall be my people.

Covenant now written on our hearts:
How is the covenant written on our hearts? It is written on our hearts when we believe in Jesus Christ and receive his Holy Spirit to dwell in us, in our hearts.
Galatians 4:6 And because ye are sons, God hath sent forth the Spirit of his Son into your hearts, crying, Abba, Father.

Why was a New Covenant needed?

See the Jews living under the Old covenant failed miserably at keeping all the laws under the Old Covenant, and the Gentiles —who were the outcast- without the Law, had no place in God. God in his grace and mercy said, I will make a better covenant to replace the Old Covenant that will not abolish the laws but fulfill them for the Jews and also make a bridge for the Gentiles to be accepted to God as well, so there will no longer be a difference between the Jew and the Gentile. God will accept them both.

So God came in flesh to dwell amongst us through his Son Jesus, in whom is the New Covenant. The New Covenant states that by Christ are all laws fulfilled by the death and resurrection of Christ. Now rather than trying to keep each law by the letter, which the Jews were not doing, all they now had to do was one thing,believe on the Son of God-Jesus Christ, and receive his Holy Spirit and they would be righteous always before God. The Gentiles now, also could come to God by doing the same thing and they too would be like the Jews-saved and righteous always before God.

Read Hebrews Chapters 8-10 For a better understanding of moving from the Old to the New covenant of God. The new covenant is by Christ, where the laws have been written on our hearts by Christ dwelling in our hearts through his Holy Spirit.

A better covenant -Hebrews 8: 6-9;13 But now hath he obtained a more excellent ministry, by how much also he is the mediator of a better covenant, which was established upon better promises. For if that first covenant had been faultless, then should no place have been sought for the second. For finding fault with them, he saith Behold, the days come saith the Lord, When I will make a new covenant with the house of Israel and with the house of Judah. Not according to the covenant that I made with their fathers in the day when I took them by the hand to lead them out of the Land of Egypt, because they continued not in my covenant, and I regarded them not saith the Lord. **v.13** In that he saith. A new covenant, he hath made the first old. Now that which decayedth and waxeth old is ready to vanish away.

Let's compare the Old Covenant to the New Covenant on the areas of:

1. **Tithing**
2. **Blessings, and Cursings**
3. **Circumcision**
4. **Sabbath**
5. **Traditions**
6. **Refraining from eating of certain meats, to show what Christ has delivered us from**

Tithes and offerings:

The following Chapter has been used most in teaching the ordinance of Tithing and offerings.

Malachi 3:6-12

The teaching that there is blessings if we bring them, and there is cursings if we don't bring them. For it says it right there. God said it. He said you are robbing him if we are not paying tithe and bringing offerings. He said he does not change. He is the same forever.

How in error again we have been teaching this.

Let's first go back to Chapter 3:1-2 God was warning them a day was coming, he was sending a messenger (foreshadow reference to John, the Baptist, for in this same book of Malachi Chapter 4:5 says he will send Elijah before that day, And we know Elijah was John the Baptist before the day of Christ coming) and then the Lord, whom you seek shall suddenly come to his temple, even the messenger of the covenant whom ye delight in: behold, he shall come, saith the Lord of hosts. And correction will begin. Continue to read verses 3 and 5.

Then in v 6-12 –God is not speaking to us today, after Christ. He is speaking to the Jews then, who were not keeping his laws well at all. They were being disobedient. He started his rebuke with Malachi Chapter 1 and Chapter 2. Go back and read them.

Now in Chapter 3: v 1-5 He is foreshadowing, telling them of the Day when John will come preparing the way for Christ. In that day they will have no out. They will be dealt with if they reject the Lord Christ.

Then he picks back up with his rebukes **in v. 6-12**, telling them about another law they were breaking, because they were playing slow, as if they did not understand what they had been doing, even after everything he had already listed in Chapters 1 and 2. You know the kid caught with chocolate all over his face, but swears he has not done anything wrong. He continues his rebuke for them. He continues now with the law of tithe and offering. How they were breaking the law of bringing the tithe and offering to the temple, and if they did not correct this, they would be cursed and not blessed. He continued to tell them how he would bless them if they did repent and turn back to bringing the tithe and offerings.

Also, let's look at the following verse in more detail.

v.6 For I am the Lord, I change not; therefore ye sons of Jacob are not consumed.

It has been taught God meant he does not change, therefore the tithe and offerings are still to be brought by the letter, and he will still curse us if we don't and bless us if we do. It is true. Tithe and offering are to still be brought but not by the letter, now by the Spirit, and there are still curses if we don't fulfill the law of tithe and offering. In other words, if we don't believe in Jesus Christ, we have not fulfilled the law of tithe and offering if we are still bringing 10% of our income but not a believer in Christ, and we are still under the curse of the law. When we believe in him, we have fulfilled this by the Spirit, not by the letter of the law, thereby, removing the curse of the law. Now as a believer we can bring whatever percentage God stirs my heart to give, without condemnation.

This scripture was also referring to this. He had made a promise, a covenant, an oath to Abraham, Isaac, Jacob and David. He would keep his covenant forever that he made with them. He would keep it with their generations forever. He would be their God and they would be his people forever as he promised when he brought them out of the Bondage of Egypt. He would never destroy them completely. There would always be a remnant. This covenant God made to their forefathers was the only reason he had not wiped them off the face of the earth. It was the only reason he had not destroyed them, because he is a God that does not change.

Even with Christ. He changed the method that his laws and covenant would be kept. Christ was his NEW method/covenant. He changed the method for attaining salvation and righteousness. His laws however were still fulfilled, his promises still fulfilled, through this better covenant by Christ Jesus. He truly is a God that does not change. He just makes things better and better. Glory to that. It is done through his new method- which is -by faith in Jesus Christ.

Although they were doing all kind of evil in breaking his laws including not bringing the tithe and offering, he would not consume them because of the covenant he had made with their forefather, that he promised them he would keep forever.

This was not to be used today to teach us that we had to continue to bring tithe and offering by the letter, AFTER the coming of Christ. He fulfilled the Tithe and Offering. This statement was to show them forever he will keep his covenant to their forefathers, in spite of their sinfulness against him. He is faithful forever even when we are faithless.

Then in v. 13-15 He tells them, but like with everything else, they keep refusing to turn back, and he says their words were stout/strong against HIM. He tells them, you continue to reject my words.

Then in v 16-18 The mercy of God shows up, because of the prayers of the righteous availeth much. Those who feared the Lord spake often to one another and sought the Lord in prayers and the Lord hearkened and heard them.

Then in Chapter 4 He continues to discuss the day that was coming, and what that day-The coming of Christ would mean for them as his people, as his chosen.

v. 2 But unto you that fear my name shall the The SUN (SON) of righteousness arise with healing in his wings.

** The Sun (SON) of righteousness he is referring to is JESUS CHRIST.

Then the book of Malachi ends and the Next Book-Matthew-begins-and who is mentioned in the very 1ˢᵗ verse of Matthew? JESUS CHRIST.

The Mention of the Sun (Son) - of Christ- Ends the Old testatment and Begins the New testatment. Ends the old covenant and begins the new covenant, ends the old tabernacle and begins the new tabernacle. God knows how to orchestrate things. How amazing is that.

For by Christ was the end of the Old –Covenant (Law) and the Beginning of the New Covenant (fulfillment of the Law by the Holy Spirit filling our hearts by our Belief in Christ.) God knows how to set things up perfectly. Is God amazing? Yes, he is.

<u>Matthew 1:1</u> The book of the **generation of Jesus Christ,** the son of David, the son of Abraham.

The Sun (SON) lineage is from the blood line of those God made the Covenant with. He is the beginning of the New Covenant.

<u>This is what the New Covenant said on tithing</u>

Christ is the first fruit/the tithe/the best of the best offering

As we believe in him, his dwelling in us makes us too first fruits. Glory.

<u>**SO now when you just walk in the church, you bring the tithe and offering in yourself-- not in your hand - but in your HEART--by Christ -the tithe/offering dwelling in your heart- by faith in Christ. You still should have a giving gift in your hand to be obedient to the command of God to be a blessing.**</u>

<u>Read:</u>

<u>**New-1 Corinthians 5:13**</u> But every man in his own order: Christ the firstfruits; afterward they that are Christ's at his coming.

James 1:18 Of his own will begat he us with the word of truth, that we should be a kind of firstfruits of his creatures.

Now let's look at a few other scriptures:

Matthew 23:23 Woe unto you, scribes and Pharisees, **hypocrites! for ye pay tithe of mint and anise and cummin, and have omitted the weightier *matters* of the law, judgment, mercy, and faith: these ought ye to have done, and not to leave the other undone.**

The above scriptures have been taught in error saying, yes the tithe is taught in New testament that it should be kept. Wrong. These scriptures were not Christ saying to continue to obey the law of tithing by the letter. If we read the whole chapter of Matthew 23, as well as Luke 12:42-54 You will see that Jesus was reprimanding the Jews. Jesus knew the proud hearts of the Pharisees. He knew how they loved sitting in the high places in the synagogues, loved to be greeted as Rabbi in the streets, how they loved to exalt their knowledge of the law above others, how they loved to give their large alms-(tithes, and other giving they may have given), how they loved to appear righteous men with it all together, but he said they were dead men walking.

For the Pharisees, it was all about appearances. Appearances of righteousness and Christ knew this. God sees the heart of man. He was showing them that though they tithed, they had rejected Christ-the Saviour, and by rejecting him they had omitted the weightier matters of the law: judgement, mercy and faith, that come from God by Christ. This is why he called them hypocrites.

You know the phrase "kill 2 birds with one stone"

They needed only one stone: the stone - called Jesus.

Acts 4: 10-11 - Be it known unto you all, and to all the people of Israel, that by the name of **Jesus Christ of Nazareth**, whom ye crucified, whom God raised from the dead, *even* by him doth this man stand here before you whole. **This is the stone** which was set at nought of you builders, which is become the head of the corner.

Jesus basically was telling the Pharisees in Matthew and Luke, if they had done this one thing -believed in the Son of God- they would not only acknowledge the judgement of God that they were sinful and receive his mercy, but they also would by this same thing, be keeping all the laws, because all the laws are fulfilled in Christ. They would have killed 2 birds with one stone-JESUS. They would have done one without leaving the other undone, because by Christ they all were completed or fulfilled.

They would not have had to pay the tithe of the mint, anise, cumin, rue and herbs by the letter. They would not have had to literally bring the tithes of these things to the Levitical priest, because the tithe just like the Sabbath was completed in Christ alone. So in believing in Christ is what they aught to have done. In doing so they would have been fulfilling tithe of cumin, judgement, mercy etc.

God proves to the Pharisees, he is not impressed about their tithe and money, he is concerned about who is dwelling in the heart. Is Jesus dwelling in their heart by His Spirit?

Look at the following scriptures.

New-Mark 12:41-44 And Jesus sat over against the treasury, and beheld how the people cast money into the treasury: and many that were rich cast in much. And there came a certain poor widow, and she threw in two mites, which make a farthing. And he called *unto him* his disciples, and saith unto them, Verily I say unto you, That this poor widow hath cast more in, than all they which have cast into the treasury: For all *they* did cast in of their abundance; but she of her want did cast in all that she had, *even* all her living

New-Luke 18:9-14 And spake this parable unto certain which trusted in themselves that they were righteous, and despised others: Two men went up into the temple to pray; the one a Pharisee, and the other a publican. **The Pharisee stood and prayed thus with himself, God, I thank thee that I am not as other men are extortioners, unjust, adulterers, or even this publican. I fast twice in the week, I give tithes of all that I possess.**

And the publican, standing afar off, would not lift up so much as his eyes unto heaven, but smote his breast saying God be merciful to me a sinner. I tell you, this man went down to his house justified rather than the other: for every one that exalteth himself shall be abased, and he that humbleth himself shall be exalted.

It does not sound as if God was going to open the windows of heaven based on the Pharisees praying and bragging about how good he was in paying tithes, being all prideful, and exalting himself above the other man.

However this is what we think. We think we get the Malachi blessings still by paying tithes by the letter, while our hearts and minds are all jacked up like that Pharisee's, because we have memorized (Malachi 3:8-12) No, the Malachi blessings and all blessings are by Christ alone now, and we need to thank him for that. For it means it is by his Grace not by our works as the prideful Pharisee thought it was by his works. So how is it the other man walked away justified rather than the Pharisee ,as the scripture said above. Again, by Grace not works. By the Spirit of God and not by the Letter of the Law.

Tithe paid to Melchisedec

Hebrews 7:2 To whom also Abrahram gave a tenth part of all
This scripture was being used by the apostle to show them that Jesus Christ was greater than their Father Abraham, because Abraham paid tithe/tenth to Melchisedec, signifying the lesser giving honor and worship to the greater. Since Christ was of the same priesthood as

Melchisedec. They too should be showing great worship towards the Son of God, to the Messiah, Jesus, as the highly regarded Abraham, their spiritual father showed to Melchisedec. Also, they should not hold Abraham in higher honor above Jesus. Jesus was greater than their father Abraham, just as Melchisedec was greater than Abraham.

This scripture also has been at the top to be used to say the law of tithing was to be kept, as part of new covenant. Wrong again.

If we read, **Hebrews chapter 6:20-7:28 we will see this story is an allegory of the transition from the old covenant to the new covenant. It shows the fulfillment of law for righteousness and the change of the priesthood.**

Allegory defined: A story, poem, play, picture, etc, in which the apparent meaning of the characters and events is used to symbolize a deeper moral or spiritual meaning.
(Free dictionary)

Some other allegories we find in the bible are when Abraham was giving his only promised seed, Isaac as a ransom freely, only to be raised again, just as Jesus the promised seed would come and be given as a ransom freely for the world. Another allegory was Jonah who was in the belly of the whale for 3 days to be raised again, as Jesus was in the grave for 3 days, and raised on the 3rd day.

Let's look at the key pieces dealing with the Melchisedec and Abraham allegory.

Melchisedec- described as the following in Hebrew Chapter 7:1-3
For this Melchisedec, king of Salem, priest of the most high God, who met Abraham returning from the slaughter of the kings, and blessed him; To whom also Abraham gave a tenth part of all; first being by interpretation King of Righteousness, and after that also King of Salem, which is, King of Peace. Without father, without

mother, without descent, having neither beginning of days, nor end of life; but made like unto the Son of God; abideth a priest continually.

v.9 And as I may so say, Levi also, who receiveth tithes, payed tithes in Abraham

v.11-14 If therefore perfection were by the Levitical priesthood(for under it people received the law) what further need was there that another priest should arise after the order of Melchisedec, and not be called after the order of Aaron- (not desecedant from Levitical priesthood which tithes were given) ? For the priesthood being changed, there is made of necessity a change also of the law. For he of whom these things are spoken pertaineth to another tribe, of which no man gave attendance at the altar. For it is evident that our Lord sprang out of Judah; of which tribe Moses spake nothing concerning priesthood.

v. 15 and it is yet far more evident; for that after the similitude of Melchisedec there ariseth another priest.

v.16 Who is made, not after the law of a carnal commandment, but after the power of an endless life.

We learn from the scripture above Melchisedec was all the following:

1. Priest of the Most High God
2. King of Salem-which is King of Peace
3. King of Righteousness
4. Without father, without mother, without descent
5. Having neither beginning of days, nor end of life,
6. But made like unto the Son of God
7. Abideth a priest continually

★★★Christ is all these things Today. ★★★

From this scripture:

Abraham: He represented the Levi/the Levitical Priesthood- (as it states in the scripture the Levi was in Abraham, i.e - the Levitical Priesthood was in Abraham)

Tithe: The tithe represented- the Law-All the Laws

When we see Abraham (the Levi, the Leviticial Priesthood) paying/ giving the Tithe (All the Law) to Melchisedec (the Son of God-Jesus-The King of righteousness, the King of Peace, having neither beginning of days, nor end of life, the Son of God, and a priest that abideth continually)

This was to show us the law given to Christ who has now fulfilled the law forever, and ended one priesthood, creating a new tabernacle not made by hands, and tearing down the old tabernacle made with hands and with all its carnal ordinances.

To further show the end of the old Levitical priesthood, Christ came from another tribe. He did not come from the tribe of Aaron -from which all the Levitical priest came.

Christ came from the tribe of Judah. No priest had ever come from the tribe of Judah. This again signifies the end of the Levitical Priesthood, and the beginning of a new Priesthood forever by Jesus to whom the laws were given and fulfilled. This was the end of the Old Covenant and Tabernacle and the beginning of the New Covenant and Tabernacle.

Read the following.

Hebrews 6:16 Now when people take an oath, they call on someone greater than themselves to hold them to it. And without any question that oath is binding. God also bound himself with an oath, so that those who received the promise could be perfectly sure that he would never change his mind. So God has given both his promise and his oath. These two things are unchangeable because it is impossible for God to lie. Therefore, we who have fled to him for refuge can have great confidence as we hold to the hope that lies before us. This hope is a strong and trustworthy anchor for our souls. **It leads us through the curtain into God's inner sanctuary. Jesus has already gone in there for us. He has become our <u>eternal High Priest</u> in the order of Melchizedek.**

<u>Matthew 8:4</u> And Jesus saith unto him, See thou tell no man; but go thy way, shew thyself to the priest, and offer the gift that Moses commanded, for a testimony unto them.

Jesus told the lepers to go show themselves to the priest as a testimony to them that he had arrived. The true high priest, who was able to forgive, cleanse, purify and heal, take away all sins.

<u>Hebrews 9:8-11</u> The Holy Ghost this signifying, that the way into the holiest of all was not yet made manifest, while as the first tabernacle was yet standing: **Which** *was* **a figure for the time then present,** in which were offered both gifts and sacrifices, that could not make him that did the service perfect, as pertaining to the conscience; *Which stood* only in meats and drinks, and divers washings, **and carnal ordinances, imposed** *on them* **until the time of reformation But Christ being come an high priest of good things to come, by a greater and more perfect tabernacle, not made with hands, that is to say, not of this building;**

<u>Colossians 2:8-17</u> Beware lest any man spoil you through philosophy and vain deceit, after the tradition of men, after the rudiments of the world, and not after Christ. For in him dwelleth all the fulness of the Godhead bodily. And ye are complete in him, which is the head of all principality and power: In whom also ye are circumcised with the circumcision made without hands, in putting off the body of the sins of the flesh by the circumcision of Christ: Buried with him in baptism, wherein also ye are risen with *him*

through the faith of the operation of God, who hath raised him from the dead.;And you, being dead in your sins and the uncircumcision of your flesh, hath he quickened together with him, having forgiven you all trespasses; Blotting out the handwriting of ordinances that was against us, which was contrary to us, and took it out of the way, nailing it to his cross; *And* having spoiled principalities and powers, he made a shew of them openly, triumphing over them in it.Let no man therefore judge you in meat, or in drink, or in respect of an holyday, or of the new moon, or of the sabbath *days* Which are a shadow of things to come; but the body *is* of Christ.

Ephesians 2:15 Having abolished in his flesh the enmity, *even* the law of commandments *contained* in ordinances; for to make in himself of twain one new man, *so* making peace;

This is to say that Christ in his flesh has abolished THE LAW (of commandments) contained in ordinances .

Blessings and Curses
This is how you were blessed and cursed in the Old Covenant.

Old- Blessing of obedience to the Laws Deuteronomy 5:33
Ye shall walk in all the ways which the LORD your God hath commanded you, that ye may live, and *that it may be* well with you, and *that* ye may prolong *your* days in the land which ye shall possess.

Old- Blessings of Law Deuteronomy 28:1-14 All the blessings of obedience to the laws given

Old- Cursings of Law Deuteronomy 28:15-68 All the cursings of disobedience to the laws given
Not only were they cursed for not giving the tithe, but for not keeping the Sabbath, for worship of other gods, and many, many more laws as you read.

This is how you were blessed in the New Covenant. And how we have been delivered from All curses that were in the Law.

New- *Galatians 3:13-14 CHRIST hath redeemed us from the CURSE of the LAW. Being made a curse for us: for it is written, Cursed is every one that hangeth on a tree
That the blessing of Abraham might come on the Gentiles through Jesus Christ; that we might receive the promise of the Spirit through faith.

*Ephesians 1:3 Blessed *be* the God and Father of our Lord Jesus Christ, who hath blessed us with all spiritual blessings in heavenly *places* in Christ

*2 Cor 1:20 All the promises of God are in Christ Jesus, yes and amen.

Circumcision

This is what the Old Covenant said about circumcision

Old--Genesis 17:1-13;14 And God said unto Abraham, Thou shalt keep my covenant therefore, thou, and thy seed after thee in their generations. This is my covenant, which ye shall keep, between me and you and thy seed after thee: Every man child among you shall be circumcised.
v. 14 And the uncircumcised man child whose flesh of his foreskin is not circumcised, that soul shall be cut off from his people; he hath broken my covenant.

This is what the New Covenant said about circumcision

New--Acts 15:1 And certain men which came down from Judea taught the brethren and said, Except ye be circumcised after the Manner of Moses, ye can not be saved.

<u>v. 5</u> But there rose up certain of the sect of the Pharisees which believed, saying, That it was needful to circumcise them, and to command them to keep the law of Moses.

<u>v .10 -11</u> Now therefore why tempt ye God, to put a yoke upon the neck of the disciples, which neither our fathers nor we were able to bear, But we believe that through the GRACE of the Lord Jesus Christ we shall be saved, even as they.

<u>v. 24</u> Forasmuch as we have heard, that certain which went out from us have troubled you with words, subverting your souls, saying, Ye must be circumcised, and keep the law: to whom we gave no such commandment.

1 Corinthians 7:19 Circumcision is nothing, and uncircumcision is nothing, but the keeping of the commandments of God

Was not circumcision a commandment of the law to be kept? Why is it nothing now? This is why, because Christ had come and now he was concerned only with the circumcision of the heart not of the flesh. He wanted to circumcise our heart with the indwelling of his Holy Spirit to all who would believe in him.

Sabbath:

Sabbath was a day of rest commanded by God for the Jews. They were to work 6 days and rest on the 7th day. There were even Sabbath years-every 7th year. God gave example of himself who created the world in 6 days and rested on the 7th day. He worked and he rested. Great example for us to keep from burn out. He looked at all he had accomplished in his work and said it was all Good. Awesome. That is the work ethic we all should have. We do things with such a spirit of excellency and then when we complete it, we too can say I did that, It is all good.

The Sabbath was considered a day that no person or animal was to do any sort of work. It was also a day of reflection on looking at all by the hand of God he had allowed them to accomplish, and thank God for it all. It was a requirement commanded or the penalty would be death . It was to be a holy day unto the Lord. A blessed day to reflect on the relationship between the Jews and their heavenly Father for all he had blessed them with and to fellowship with other believers in God for his marvelous works in their lives. It was a day to set aside as sanctified and consecrated before God.

Today many view the Sabbath day as Sunday–because this is the day we usually assemble in our church homes to fellowship with other believers to lift up our praises to our Lord and to bring our tithe and offerings and gifts of giving. It is the day we have set aside as holy unto God. This is great and commanded by God that we forsake not the assembling of ourselves with other believers and we should continue to do this.

Today we know that some people work on Sundays. It is required by their employer. This is the job God has blessed them with. Many times they have been condemned by others for having to work on Sunday and told they may need to find another job. Some of us still wash cars, do laundry, and many other chores that we may not have had the opportunity to complete during the week. We start them before Sunday service and finish them up after Sunday service. Many have been told they should not be doing this on a Sunday. Which is also not correct. It is legalistic.
There are also some who just choose not to attend church at all in order to go golfing, etc.
They too have been condemned as not keeping the Sabbath. Which is also not correct.

We will see as we get into the scriptures that God basically told the Pharisees and Sadducees that he is not holding it against anyone that has to work on Sunday. He is not holding it against anyone that does chores and errands after they get home on Sunday or even before they go to church on Sunday. He is not holding them accountable even if they go golfing, sometimes. These are just legalities we use that condemn one another. I remember back in the day, you couldn't watch tv, or go to the movies, and women were told they could not wear pants, or makeup. It was considered unholy. Really. It was legalistic.

We will see Jesus and the disciples working and healing on the Sabbath day and being told they were breaking the law of God.

What Jesus was trying to show the Pharisees and Sadducees was to get from under the legalistics of the law. He had come and now he was the Sabbath. He was feeding his hungry disciples. He was being a blessing to them. He was again all the law fulfilled-even the Sabbath. He was the one that has been set aside as our rest which is why he said let all who are heavy laden come to him and find rest for their weary soul. He was the one set aside for us, sanctified for us and he is the one who sanctifies, justifies, and consecrates us, for his good use. It is to Him we should come in fellowship and relationship with for all that he has done for us through his life. He wants us to enter into this rest with him. It is Him the-Lord of the Sabbath-the Lord of rest forever, that we needed. He again was trying to show them that the keeping of the Sabbath was no longer by the letter but by the Spirit in your heart. Which is why he did not feel condemned by the Pharisees or the Sadducees when he allowed his disciples to pick the grain or when he himself healed the man with the shriveled hand.

Yes, God wants us to take time for ourselves to refresh, renew, be revived in body, soul, and spirit. We cannot run and run without getting physical rest. Yes, we should attend Church for we need relationship with other believers. We need to assemble in the sanctuary to hear the word of the Lord, and bring our worship. We need to continue to be taught in the word of God that we may grow in faith and in the knowledge of Jesus Christ. Yes. Yes. Yes. All that. However, the greatest Sabbath is in believing in Jesus Christ and entering into our Rest with him forever, while we live in our temporal bodies on this earth, as well as when we live in heaven for our eternal life.

This is what the Old Covenant said about Sabbath
Old--Exodus 31:12-15 And the Lord spoke to Moses saying Speak thou also to the children of Israel, saying, Verily my Sabbaths you shall keep for it is a sign between me and you throughout your generations that you may know that I am the Lord that doth sanctify you. You shall keep the Sabbath therefore for it is holy unto you. Everyone that defileth it shall surely be put to death; for whosoever doeth any work therein that soul shall be cut off from among his people. Six days may work be done; but in the seventh is the Sabbath of rest, holy to the Lord; whosoever doeth any work in the sabath day, he shall surely be put to death

Old-- Deuteronomy 5:12-14 Observe the sabbath day to keep it holy, as the LORD your God commanded you. Six days thou shalt labour, and do all thy work, but the seventh day *is* the sabbath of the LORD thy God: *in it* thou shalt not do any work, thou, nor thy son, nor thy daughter, nor thy manservant, nor thy maidservant, nor thine ox, nor thine ass, nor any of thy cattle, nor thy stranger that *is* within thy gates; that thy manservant and thy maidservant may rest as well as thou

The following 2 scriptures will be for reference to what Jesus says to the Pharisees on the Sabbath when the Pharisees believe his disciples are breaking the Sabbath in Luke and Matthew, that we will see in the next section.

Old-1 Samuel 21:4-6 Shew bread given to david and the men .
And the priest answered David and said, there is no common bread under mine hand, but there is hallowed bread, if the young men have kept themselves at least from women. And David answered the priest, and said unto him, of a truth women have been kept from us about 3 days since I came out and the vessels of the young men are holy, and the bread is in a manner common, yea though it were

sanctified this day in the vessel so the priest gave him hallowed bread; for there was no bread there but the showbread that was taken from before the Lord, to put hot bread in the day when it was taken away.

Old -Leviticus 22:10 There shall no stranger, eat of the holy thing, a sojourner of the priest, or an hired servant shall not eat of the holy thing

This is what the New Covenant said about the Sabbath

(refer back to the previous 1 Samuel 21:4-6 and Leviticus 22:10) as you read the following scriptures:

New--Read Luke 6:1-11 There was a time, the same Pharisees tried to condemn Jesus and his disciples for eating food from the corn fields on the Sabbath, and Jesus for healing on the Sabbath, for they said it too was unlawful based on law. When he got through with them, they were mad and sought to destroy him.

And they are seeking to destroy and discredit God's teachers today as well.

New-- Luke 6:1-5 And it came to pass on the Sabbath after the first, that he went through the corn fields and his disciples plucked the ears of corn, and did eat, rubbing them in their hands. And certain of the Pharisees said unto them, Why do ye that which is not lawful to do on the Sabbath days? And Jesus answering them said, Have ye not read so much as this, what David did, when himself was a hungered, and they which were with him; How he went into the house of God, and did take and eat he the showbread, and gave also to them that were with him; which it is not lawful to eat but for the priests alone? And he said unto them, That the Son of man is Lord also of the Sabbath.

New--Matthew 12:9-14 And when he departed thence, he went into their synagogue; And behold, there was a man which had his hand withered. And they asked him saying, Is it lawful to heal on the Sabbath days? That they might accuse him. And he said unto them, What man shall there be among you, that shall have one sheep, and if it fall into a pit on the Sabbath day, will he not lay hold on it, and lift it out? How much then is a man better than a sheep? Wherefore it is lawful to do well on the Sabbath days. Then saith he to the man, Stretch forth thine hand. And he stretched it forth; and it was restored whole, like as the other. Then the Pharisees went out, and held a council against him, how they might destroy him.

Remember the Sabbath was considered to be holy, a day of rest for the Lord's people, and animals and land. No work of any kind was to be done on the Sabbath, yet while the Pharisees were trying to trap Jesus, he turned it on them again, and told the Pharisees, you all are trying to condemn me who is the Sabbath. I am not one day of rest. I am 365 days of rest and an Eternal rest for your weary souls. This law and all the laws are fulfilled in me Christ.

New- John 5:15-18 The man departed, and told the Jews that it was Jesus, which had made him whole. And therefore did the Jews persecute Jesus, and sought to slay him, because he had done these things on the sabbath day. But Jesus answered them, My Father worketh hitherto, and I work. Therefore the Jews sought the more to kill him, because he not only had broken the sabbath, but said also that God was his Father, making himself equal with God.

New-- John 9:16 Therefore said some of the Pharisees, This man is not from God for he does not keep the Sabbath day. Others said how can a man that is a sinner do such miracles? And there was a division among them

See again nothing new under the sun. In the bible, it was being said he was not from God because he did not keep the Sabbath. They were not willing to accept that He was the Sabbath. They are saying the same thing about teachers today who are teaching that you do not have to keep the Sabbath by the letter, yes you can work on a job on Sunday if that is what God calls you to do to provide for your family, etc. without cursings and condemnation and you do not have to pay the tithe by the letter, or you do not have to be circumcised by the letter, because it is accomplished by the Spirit by Grace. They are saying these teachers of the gospel are not from God. They are breaking the Law. We see this is the same thing they said about Christ who was teaching the same thing of fulfillment and Grace. They said the same thing about Paul and all Pastors, teachers, Evangelists, and disciples who teach truth of Grace of God concerning the tithe. We see Pastors and leaders going against one another because one thinks the one is right or wrong. God said neither way is wrong. One is law and one is Grace. One is of a believer who has not matured to understand the Grace of teaching of tithe over the Law teaching. We must be obedient to God as he said in Romans chapter 14 to not get into dispute over matters like this. Walk together as each of us continue to grow in him. No one is sinning in this area. Both are doing it unto God whether by understanding of Law or understanding of Grace. God will bring the one who is still under the bondage of the Law to better understanding in his own time. Until that time. Let us be obedient to God to walk in love not strife and dispute over this subject.

Whose report will you believe, Man's or God's? I believe God's. Who will you obey, Man or God? I choose to obey God.

Acts 4:19 But Peter and John answered and said unto them, Whether it be right in the sight of God to hearken unto you more than unto God, judge ye.

Whose approval do we desire. Man or God. Let it always be to meet the approval of God. Let us not love the approval or praise of Man over God's.

Traditions

The following will be scripture references to what is discussed about washen hands/ and the Corban in the New Testament

Old-Mother and Father Corban Deuteronomy 5:16 Honour thy father and thy mother, as the LORD thy God hath commanded thee; that thy days may be prolonged, and that it may go well with thee, in the land which the LORD thy God giveth thee

Old- Washen hands –before eating holy food. This was from Leviticus 22:5-7 Or whosoever toucheth any creeping thing, whereby he may be made unclean, or a man of whom he may take uncleanness, **whatsoever uncleanness he hath; The soul which hath touched any such shall be unclean until even, and shall not eat of the holy thinks, unless he wash his flesh with water. And when the sun is down, he shall be clean, and shall afterward eat of the holy things; because it *is* his food.**

New—Washen hands Mark 7:5-14 Then the Pharisees and scribes asked him, Why walk not thy disciples according to the tradition of the elders, but eat bread with unwashen hands?

He answered and said unto them, Well hath Esaias prophesied of you hypocrites, as it is written, This people honoureth me with their lips, but their hearts is far from me. Howbeit in vain do they worship me, teaching for doctrines the commandments of men.

For laying aside the commandment of God, ye hold the tradition of men, as the washing of pots and cups; and many other such like things ye do. And he said unto them, Full well ye reject the commandment of God, that ye may keep your own traditions.

For Moses said Honour thy father and thy mother; and whoso curseth father or mother, let him die the death. But ye say, if a man shall say to his father or mother, it is Corban, that is to say, a gift, by whatsoever thou mightiest be profited by me: he shall be free. And ye suffer him no more to do ought for his father or his mother; making the word of God of none effect through your tradition, which ye have delivered: and many such like things do ye. And when he had called the people unto him, he said unto them, Hearken unto me every one of you, and understand.

God clearly tells the Pharisees here, that in keeping their own generational traditional teachings, they have in fact, rejected the commandment of God given to the Jews by the Mosaic Law in the above Deuteronomy 5:16 scripture, by teaching the people to not give to their parents which were in need. This had been taught and passed down through the generations. This is the same thing being done today through traditional generational teaching concerning the tithe and offering, sabbath, pants in the church, make up in the church, women teachers in the church, etc and so on. It is taught if you pay your mortgage or use the tithe to help another in any way you will be cursed according to the law. This has been taught wrong, as God has proven here. Thank God for the generational traditional teachings, it covered us, but now that God is shedding more light today on his truths, let us arise and move forward in his newness of mind, in this renewed mind he is giving us.

Trust me I admit I taught some things wrong over my years of teaching, Thank God for grace. Today he has blessed me to teach correctly many of those things that were taught in error, and as I continue to grow from faith to faith, and glory to glory and as God gives me new revelations daily as he helps me to rightly divide his word as I become his willing and obedient servant to deny myself daily and pick up my cross daily and follow him, as he teaches me more about his Grace. As he renews my mind daily. And as he strengthens me daily to follow him and walk in the newness of my renewed mind. God is doing a new thing. Do you not perceive it. Glory to God.

In the bible, Christ called them hypocrites because they were trying to condemn him and his disciples about eating with unwashen hands, when in fact they too, under the Law was breaking the Law concerning Honoring one's mother and father.

Meats

This is what the Old Testament said about what meats could or could not be eaten

Old-- Deuteronomy 14:3 -21 Read about the meats that could and could not be eaten

This is what the New Testament said about the meats

New: Mark 7:18 -23 And he saith unto them, Are ye so without understanding also? Do ye not perceive, that whatsoever thing from without entereth into the man, *it* cannot defile him; Because it entereth not into his heart, but into the belly, and goeth out into the draught, purging all meats? And he said, That which cometh out of the man, that defileth the man. For from within, out of the heart of men, proceed evil thoughts, adulteries, fornications, murders, Thefts, covetousness, wickedness, deceit, lasciviousness, an evil eye, blasphemy, pride, foolishness. All these evil things come from within, and defile the man.

New-1 Timothy 4:1,3-5 Now the Spirit speaketh expressly, that in the latter times some shall depart from the faith, giving heed to seducing spirit, and doctrines of devils; .. Forbidding to marry, and commanding to abstain from meats, which God hath created to be received with thanksgiving of them which believe and know the truth. **For every creature of God is good, and nothing to be refused, if it be received with thanksgiving: For it is sanctified by the word of God and prayer.**

Thank the Lord for your meal, Pray over your food and bon appetit. Eat what you like, and don't eat what you don't like. Always, Always do all things in moderation.

New- 1 Corinthians 8:7-9
Howbeit *there is* **not in every man that knowledge**: for some with conscience of the idol unto this hour eat *it* as a thing offered unto an idol; and their conscience being weak is defiled. But meat commendeth us not to God:

for neither, if we eat, are we the better

neither, if we eat not, are we the worse

But take heed lest by any means this liberty of yours become a stumbling block to them that are weak.

This is the argument over the issue of tithing, and many other subjects of the bible. Some feel they will be better off if they do it by the letter and will be worse off if they did it by Grace. Others who know they are under New Covenant know they are no better off if they do it, and no Worse if they don't do it by the letter. However, they know they must believe in Christ.

These issues also deal with our spiritual growth- the weaker/babe Christian and stronger/more mature Christian comes into discussion.

God does not want the weaker and the stronger Christian to get into strife over these things. God tells the stronger Christian to be careful as well to not be a stumbling block to the weaker Christian, or to the weaker unbeliever. He did not say the stronger Christian was wrong in his beliefs. He just wanted to say don't argue over these things even when you know you are right. Respect your weaker brethren views and vice versa. Don't be a stumbling block to one another.

So for those who want to say, no, no, no. One of them is sinning, one of them is wrong, and one is right. Nope. You are Wrong for saying that. It does not matter to God either way, because neither of them is wrong, neither of them is sinning. The only difference is one is stronger and one is weaker in their understanding and administration of the Grace of God on the issue of tithing and meats and other laws. He is the fulfillment of the law and he has set you free from having to do certain parts of it to the letter. Doing the law by the letter is not bad. The Law is good. It is not sin. You will not be punished or chastised for it, but he wants you to live in His grace. Live in the freedom he has provided by his Son.

It is the Law that shows you the need for Grace and Mercy by Christ.

We see he has fulfilled the Sabbath, Passover, observance of Moons, and many other Festivals and days, Tithe and Offerings, Levitical priesthood, and many other things they were commanded to observe
The Jews could not accept this
The Jews could not accept this. Many did not believe in Christ and turned from him. The Jews chose to continue under the Old way to righteousness which was under the Law by the letter instead of believing in Christ for their righteousness. Since, Christ was rejected by the Jews, he then turned to the Gentiles, making salvation available to all. Now there would be no difference between the Jew or the Gentile.

If they accepted Christ and still wanted to bring tithe and offerings and observe Sabbath days. That would be their choice. To continue to do the carnal ordinances by the letter was no longer a requirement AFTER CHRIST, but to walk in love with one another was still commanded.

When Christ came he fulfilled them ALL by the Spirit. In his fulfilling them all by his Spirit meant this:

He still commanded us to continue to walk in love and do good to one another, maintain good works. It pretty much means I still require you to not steal and not kill and still require you to be fair in business, and honor your father and mother, and not commit adultery, i.e. walk in love, show and do good to one another, give money, give time, give, give, give. But I don't require that you bring burnt offerings, grain offerings, animal blood sacrifices, tithe offerings by the letter, and I don't require you observe certain festivals and days, I don't require that only the priests can come before the throne and mercy seat for you, you can come behind the veil to the mercy seat to my throne yourself. This is what I, God, did by Grace, through my Son, Jesus Christ for you.

That is simple.

So why are we still living under the Law and not under his Grace.

★★★NOTE: To get a thorough understanding of the law and it carnal ordinances and other requirements, please read the books of Genesis through Deuteronomy that details all the law, regulations, ordinances, including morality laws, civil laws, lending laws, property laws, the Ten Commandments, requirements of offerings, and worship for the priests, and service to the tabernacle, requirements of festivals and days etc. under the Old Tabernacle and under the Old Covenant.

I know you may be still be confused. I hope not, but I can understand, because so was I when God began to show me these things. I promise you, he will make it plain. Ask him to give you understanding, and he will.

2 Timothy 2:7 Consider what I say; and the Lord give thee understanding in all things

This is what Paul and the Pharisees division was about also, and is still the same today. Nothing new under the Sun.

Ecclesiastes 1:9-10 The thing that hath been, it is that which shall be; and that which is done is that which shall be done, and there is no new thing under the sun. Is there anything whereof it may be said, See, this is new? It hath been already of old time, which was before us.

Lets look at some of the questions that Paul explained as he taught the Pharisees about how Christ had come and fulfilled the Laws. The same things that are being asked and said today when the teachings about the law and grace comes into discussion.

In the book of Romans and Galatians, Paul was explaining to the Pharisees and Sadducees, and Gentiles, that Christ was the end to the law for righteousness.

In the Book of Romans, Chapters 1 through 3, have so often been used as scriptures to teach the righteous about how they will be turned over to reprobate minds and not inherit the kingdom of God after being saved through Christ. This has been incorrect.

In these chapters Paul is speaking to 2 groups. Those who have placed their faith in Christ, Jews or Gentiles, and those who have not placed their faith in Christ, Jews and Gentiles.

To the 1st group, he addresses as brethren in the faith of Jesus Christ their Lord. He rebukes and chastises them. Informing them who have the faith of Jesus and is sinning will be judged by God for their sinful acts, harshly, if they do persist on sinning. None is to think that God will not judge them for their sins made in this body. Judgement and Chastisement does not mean they will lose their salvation and are condemned to hell. However, who wants to be judged harshly by God while we live or die. Paul wanted his fellow believers to repent and turn back to their righteous ways.

Paul is also speaking to a 2ⁿᵈ group. This group is to his brethren, his fellow Jews who have not believed on Christ, as well to other Gentiles that also have not believed in Christ. This group will also be judged in the same way as the 1ˢᵗ group, no difference, in the judgement, both groups will face God in the judgement, but there is a difference in the condemnation. This group will not inherit the kingdom of God, they will be condemned to hell forever.

This is why Paul was persuading them to turn their lives over to Christ, for yes all will have to give account for their sins in the body. For we all will be counted as having fallen short before God and sinned. This is what Paul is teaching in the Book of Romans chapter 3. Thanks be to God that by Christ and believing in him we will not be condemned to hell forever, we can still enter into the kingdom of God -by Christ forever.

Romans 8:1-3 *There is* therefore now no condemnation to them which are in Christ Jesus, who walk not after the flesh, but after the Spirit. For the law of the Spirit of life in Christ Jesus hath made me free from the law of sin and death. For what the law could not do, in that it was weak through the flesh, God sending his own Son in the likeness of sinful flesh, and for sin, condemned sin in the flesh:

In the Book of Romans Chapter 1 through 3 Paul rebukes the Jew and the Gentile, the one with the law and without the law. He tells the Jews yes they are correct in what they say about the Gentile who are without the law and doing all types of evil before God without the law, and will not inherit the kingdom of God if they do not turn to God. He also rebukes the Jews and tells them, who had the Law of God-Mosaic law. You are no better than them, for you are doing the same thing as them and think that you are still justified for the Kingdom of God through the Mosaic Law, and Father Abraham, but there is a greater one than Abraham that has come. He told them neither the Gentile or Jew that broke the law would be justified before God. Neither of them that rejects Jesus- The fulfillment of the

Law will ever be justified before God. Only those who kept the Law by faith in Jesus would be justified before God . All will be chastised and judged for their deeds in the body. All will die for their sins, but after death of the grave, all will be raised for a final judgement. This Is the judgment that if your name is not in the book of Life because of your faith in Jesus, You will be condemned to hell forever.

Now they were smitten, what was Paul saying. Here he had grouped them all alike, Jew and Gentile. If neither kept the law, neither would enter the kingdom of God. What was this new teaching Paul had? It was the teaching of the Gospel of Jesus Christ as Paul opens **in Romans 3:20-31** –The only way now that either can be justified before God is by –Christ alone.

Romans 3:20-31 Therefore by the deeds of the law there shall no flesh be justified in his sight: for by the law *is* the knowledge of sin. **But now the righteousness of God without the law is manifested,** being witnessed by the law and the prophets; **Even the righteousness of God** *which is* **by faith of Jesus Christ unto all and upon all them that believe:** for there is no difference: For all have sinned, and come short of the glory of God Being justified freely by his grace through the redemption that is in Christ Jesus Whom God hath set forth *to be* a propitiation through faith in his blood, to declare his righteousness for the remission of sins that are past, through the forbearance of God; To declare, *I say*, at this time his righteousness: that he might be just, and the justifier of him which believeth in Jesus. Where *is* boasting then? It is excluded. By what law? of works? Nay: but by the law of faith. Therefore we conclude that a man is justified by faith without the deeds of the law. *Is he* the God of the Jews only? *is he* not also of the Gentiles? Yes, of the Gentiles also: Seeing *it is* one God, which shall justify the circumcision by faith, and uncircumcision through faith.
Do we then make void the law through faith? God forbid: yea, we establish the law.

Paul in the following were teaching them that we are now justified and approved through Christ alone.

Romans 10:3-5 For they being ignorant of God's righteousness, and going about to establish their own righteousness, have not submitted themselves unto the righteousness of God. For Christ *is* the end of the law for righteousness to every one that believeth. For Moses describeth the righteousness which is of the law

Galatians 3:23-26 But before faith came, we were kept under the law, shut up unto the faith which should afterwards be revealed. Wherefore the law was our schoolmaster *to bring us* unto Christ, that we might be justified by faith. But after that faith is come, we are no longer under a schoolmaster. For ye are all the children of God by faith in Christ Jesus

However, they refused to accept what Paul was saying. Let's look at a few questions Paul addressed, and notice if any sound familiar today.

So Paul what are you saying? If what you are saying is true Paul that Christ has made the Jew and the Gentile alike, no difference,
What advantage then hath the Jew? Or what profit is there of circumcision? Romans 3:1

In Romans 3:3 -8 Paul goes on to explain to them that God is truth, he can not lie. The Jews are still the chosen of God. Paul goes on to explain to the Jews don't get it twisted. Their chosen status is not their card for right standing before God. The chosen group has to believe on Christ as well, or they are still unrighteous in his eyes because their keeping the law without faith in Jesus will not save them and will not keep them in right standing before God any longer. Those who do not believe on Christ even from the Chosen, the Elect group –the Jews will feel the vengeance of God. He will not overlook their unrighteousness. He will not overlook their rejecting Christ because they think they are righteous before him by the law and because they are the Chosen. He will not allow them to trample under foot His Son, Jesus Christ. No, that would be their mistake. That would be like God telling the Jews do evil and receive good from him. God will not allow this. He would not allow them to do the evil of not receiving Christ and think that good will be towards them. He will judge them. They would be condemned. The sin of rejecting the Son of God as Lord and Saviour is blasphemy of the Holy Spirit that can not be forgiven. All other sins can be forgiven, now punishment and chastisement of these other sins is based on whether God chooses to have mercy or not. Remember his grace is sufficient even with his afflictions.

Then in Romans 3:9-10 Paul continues to clear up some misconceptions. So Jews, What then? Are we better then they (the Gentiles) because we are the chosen? Paul says no, in no wise for all are under sin, for it is written there is none righteous, no not one. You and I are not superior to another.

Romans 3:31 Paul continues. Do we then make void the law through faith? God forbid: yea, we establish the law.
Paul was asking the Pharisees do you think we are voiding out the laws. Making them null and void, useless. No. He says, we are establishing/fulfilling the law through Christ.

Romans 5:20- 6:2 Moreover the law entered, that the offence might abound. But where sin abounded, grace did much more abound: That as sin hath reigned unto death, even so might grace reign through righteousness unto eternal life by Jesus Christ our Lord. **What shall we say then? Shall we continue in sin, that grace may abound. God forbid,** How shall we, that are dead to sin, live any longer therein?

Paul was telling them, you do not have a license to sin, because you are under grace. You must still let brotherly love continue and obey the guidance of the Holy Spirit and

not yield your members to the flesh and its lusts. **Not having to do these particular carnal ordinances of festivals, grain offerings, by the letter, does not give you permission to hate, steal, kill, and all other evils and lust of the heart and eyes. We as people of God must learn how to rightly divide the word so we can discern what God is truly speaking and the way we do so is by prayer for discernment and understanding and for the veils to be removed from our minds, eyes and ears so that we may know, see and hear what he is speaking as his truths as we study. Amen**

Romans 6:15 What then? Shall we sin, because we are not under the law, but under grace? God forbid.
The previous scripture is scripture that pertains to the same thing people are saying today. They said it back then. They said so Paul, you are saying, we should sin more to receive more grace? Are you saying since we are not under the law, we have license to sin since grace has come, for Grace by Christ covers it all.

Paul said God forbid, no, I am not saying that. I am telling you that when you believe on Christ you are buried and raised in the newness of life – a life that is hidden in Christ-in whom there is no sin-the body of sin has been destroyed by the Spirit of Christ. V.17 he tells them before we believed in Christ we were servants who yielded our members to sin, but thanks be to God, since we have obeyed from the heart that was given to us about receiving Christ, we have been made free from sin, and become the servants of righteousness by grace not by our continuous shortcomings. This is why Paul goes on to say in Chapter 7:24 O wretched man am I, who keeps falling and not able to do that which I would want to do good. The only way he was delivered was by Christ. If God keeps looking at us instead of Christ in whom our lives are now hid, we would never measure up. We have to think like God, not in the carnal mind, but in the spiritual mind, that God is looking at the Saviour not at you and I. Then we are children yielding our members to the righteousness of

God and not to sin-because Christ, the one the Father is looking at is Without sin forever. This is called renewing the mind and walking in that renewed mind not the carnal and flesh mind. Thinking about things in the way God thinks and sees them.

Romans 7:7 What shall we say then? Is the law sin? God forbid. Nay, I had not known sin, but by the law; for I had not known lust, except the law had said. Thou shalt not covet.
Romans 7: 12-14 Wherefore the law is holy, and the commandment holy, and just, and good. Was then that which is good made death unto me? God forbid. But sin, that it might appear sin, working death in me by that which is good; that sin by the commandment might become exceeding sinful For we all know that the law is spiritual: but I am carnal, sold under sin.

They were asking Paul. Do you mean you are saying, if we keep tithing by the letter or keep observing the Sabbath and Passover, or keep with the various offerings, etc. that we are sinning. Did God administer sin, when he gave the Law to us. Paul said No. God forbid. God gave the law to show us his love and grace for us even then, and to show us ourselves, just how sinful we are in nature. He also showed us that he loved us so much he would later prepare a better way for his people. God has fulfilled all these things by Christ. God was working his plan from the beginning. The plan of Love, Grace, Mercy, Resurrection with Power, Redemption and Restoration and Eternal Life while we were yet sinners .

Paul explains here that many may have been thinking now, Paul are you saying that teaching the law is sin? You are saying the law is sin? Paul said no again. He said the law was good, just and holy. It was used to show us how miserable we were at keeping the law which is why Christ had to come. It was used to show us how sinful we were that it may bring us to come to the end of ourselves, so that we choose to be baptized into Jesus Christ thereby being baptized into his death. Therefore, as we are buried with him by baptism into death; that like as Christ was raised up from the dead by the glory of the Father, even so we also should walk in the newness of life. For if we have been planted together in the likeness of his death, we shall be also in the likeness of his resurrection. Knowing this, that our old man is crucified with him, that the body of sin might be destroyed, that henceforth we should not serve sin - **as stated in Romans 6:3-6.**

Romans 9:14-16 What shall we say then? *Is there* **unrighteousness with God? God forbid**. For he saith to Moses, I will have mercy on whom I will have mercy, and I will have compassion on whom I will have compassion. So then *it is* not of him that willeth, nor of him that runneth, but of God that sheweth mercy.

It was based on grace and mercy of God not on the works of the law.

Galatians 2:16-17 Knowing that a man is not justified by the works of the law, but by the faith of Jesus Christ, even we have believed in Jesus Christ, that we might be justified by the faith of Christ, and not by the works of the law: for by the works of the law shall no flesh be justified. But if, while we seek to be justified by Christ, we ourselves also are found sinners, *is* **therefore Christ the minister of sin? God forbid.**

Paul teachings were rejected and he was seen as one against God as many who teach fulfillment and Grace by faith in Christ are today: Read the following:

Acts 21:17-30 And when we were come to Jerusalem, the brethren received us gladly. And the *day* following Paul went in with us unto James; and all the elders were present. And when he had saluted them, he declared particularly what things God had wrought among the Gentiles by his ministry. And when they heard *it*, they glorified the Lord, and said unto him, Thou seest, brother, how many thousands of Jews there are which believe; and they are all zealous of the law: And they are informed of thee, that thou teachest all the Jews which are among the Gentiles to forsake Moses, saying that they ought not to circumcise *their* children, neither to walk after the customs. What is it therefore? the multitude must needs come together: for they will hear that thou art come. Do therefore this that we say to thee: We have four men which have a vow on them; Them take, and purify thyself with them, and be at charges with them, that they may shave *their* heads: and all may know that those things, whereof they were informed concerning thee, are nothing; but *that* thou thyself also walkest orderly, and keepest the law. As touching the Gentiles which believe, we have written *and* concluded that they observe no such thing, save only that they keep themselves from *things* offered to idols, and from blood, and from strangled, and from fornication. Then Paul took the men, and the next day purifying himself with them entered into the temple, to signify the accomplishment of the days of purification, until that an offering should be offered for every one of them. And when the seven days were almost ended, the Jews which were of Asia, when they saw him in the temple, stirred up all the people, and laid hands on him, Crying out, Men of Israel, help: **This is the man, that teacheth all *men* every where against the people, and the law, and this place: and further brought Greeks also into the temple, and hath polluted this holy place. (For they had seen before with him in the city Trophimus an Ephesian, whom they supposed that Paul had brought into the temple.) And all the city was moved, and the people ran together: and they took Paul, and drew him out of the temple: and forthwith the doors were shut.**

Paul answered them as God led him to, but they still could not grasp what Paul was saying. Just because they could not grasp it, does not mean Paul's teachings were not truth.

Do you see now, what God means, there is nothing new under the Sun. We are experiencing the same type of discussions/debates/strivings even today, because it is hard for people to grasp the concept of his Great Grace and fulfillment

The Pharisees had a hard time accepting what Paul was teaching. They also felt Paul did not know more than them about the laws. However, Paul knew the laws well. He had been a persecutor of the church. He believed, at one time, that the gospel of Grace and Faith by Christ, was against the Laws he and the Pharisees knew well. Now that Jesus had come into Paul's life, he understood the Grace and Fulfillment of the Messiah. Now the thinking he once had about the law was changed with his knowledge of Jesus. His mission before was to persecute anyone who chose to follow after the Grace of God by believing in Christ as Lord.

That was until he met GOD on his Damascus Road.

Let us be as Paul did and as commanded by our God in his word:

2 Peter 3:18 But grow in grace, and in the knowledge of our Lord and Saviour Jesus Christ. To him be glory both now and for ever. Amen
One thing Paul did know more than the Pharisees and Sadduccees after his Damascus Road experience was the Grace of God that had come into his life. We should know when you have been in the presence of God he is able to make the wise look foolish and the strong look weak. This is what was occurring. Paul had been in the presence of the Most High that had taught him what the Pharisees could not understand.

Read:

1 Corinthians 1:27- But God hath chosen the foolish things of the world to confound the wise; and God hath chosen the weak things of the world to confound the things which are mighty;

Read also -1 Corinthians 1:17-30 and Galatians 2:21

The Pharisees also could not figure out where all Jesus knowledge came from either at age 12, when he was teaching in the temple courts, or when his adult ministry begin. They could not understand how the son of a carpenter had such wisdom. It's just God putting on display All that he is, in all his glory. Amen.

Read the following about how hard it was for them to accept the wisdom of Christ:

Luke 2:46-47 And it came to pass, that after three days they found him in the temple, sitting in the midst of the doctors, both hearing them, and asking them questions. And all that heard him were astonished at his understanding and answers.

Matthew 15:53-57 And it came to pass, *that* when Jesus had finished these parables, he departed thence. And when he was come into his own country, he taught them in their synagogue, insomuch that they were astonished, and said, Whence hath this *man* this wisdom, and *these* mighty works. Is not this the carpenter's son? is not his mother called Mary? and his brethren, James, and Joses, and Simon, and Judas? And his sisters, are they not all with us? Whence then hath this *man* all these things? And they were offended in him. But Jesus said unto them, A prophet is not without honour, save in his own country, and in his own house.

Jews reject Christ, Gentiles received him.

Acts 13:38-52 Be it known unto you therefore, men *and* brethren, that through this man is preached unto you the forgiveness of sins: And by him all that believe are justified from all things, from which ye could not be justified by the law of Moses. Beware therefore, lest that come upon you, which is spoken of in the prophets; Behold, ye despisers, and wonder, and perish: for I work a work in your days, a work which ye shall in no wise believe, though a man declare it unto you. And when the Jews were gone out of the synagogue, the Gentiles besought that these words might be preached to them the next sabbath. Now when the congregation was broken up, many of the Jews and religious proselytes followed Paul and Barnabas: who, speaking to them, persuaded them to continue in the grace of God. And the next sabbath day came almost the whole city together to hear the word of God. But when the Jews saw the multitudes, they were filled with envy, and spake against those things which were spoken by Paul, contradicting and blaspheming. Then Paul and Barnabas waxed bold, and said, It was necessary that the word of God should first have been spoken to you: but seeing ye put it from you, and judge yourselves unworthy of everlasting life, lo, we turn to the Gentiles. For so hath the Lord commanded us, *saying*, I have set thee to be a light of the Gentiles, that thou shouldest be for salvation unto the ends of the earth. And when the Gentiles heard this, they were glad, and glorified the word of the Lord: and as many as were ordained to eternal life believed. And the word of the Lord was published throughout all the region But the Jews stirred up the devout and honourable women, and the chief men of the city, and raised persecution against Paul and Barnabas, and expelled them out of their coasts But they shook off the dust of their feet against them, and came unto Iconium. And the disciples were filled with joy, and with the Holy Ghost.

Now there is No difference between the Jew and the Gentile- Since Christ had come. All were counted as sinful and could only be justified by Christ.

THINGS I LEARNED

DON'T REJECT THE TEACHINGS OF THE TRUTH ON THE GRACE OF CHRIST OVER THE LAW OF PAYING TITHE AND OFFERINGS BY THE LETTER.

Paul asked the Jews and Gentiles. There was a time you loved me so that you would have given both your eyes for me, he said. Now you hate me because I tell you truth?

Read:

Galatians 4:15-16
Where is then the blessedness ye spake of? for I bear you record, that, if *it had been* possible, ye would have plucked out your own eyes, and have given them to me. Am I therefore become your enemy, because I tell you the truth?

The religious leaders (Pharisees, Sadducees, Scribes) rejected Jesus as well saying, he was not of God because he was teaching them he was the fulfillment of the ordinance the Sabbath, and showing them they no longer had to observe it by the Letter.

John 9:16 Therefore said some of the Pharisees, This man is not of God, because he keepeth not the sabbath day. Others said, How can a man that is a sinner do such miracles? And there was a division among them.

Do we see the DIVISION in the body of Christ that was between JESUS CHRIST, himself, and the religious Leaders. We see this division today in the Christian community among ourselves.

Then they still rejected Paul after God sent him. The same thing. They are rejecting anyone teaching differently about the traditional law of the word because they now have their eyes opened to see what the Grace of God through faith in Jesus has truly done for us.

We as Christians are still in strife, against the Truth, against Christ, after the TRUTH has been given to them. They are still rejecting Jesus and his disciple teaching of Grace fulfillment.

They are being told they are teaching or preaching another gospel or another word or untruths.
However, we must be like Ezekiel. God told Ezekiel, I am sending you with a word to a stiffnecked stubborn and rebellious nation. Do not be afraid of their faces or words.

The same with us today who has grown to understand God's grace concerning the tithe, we must teach it correctly, as God himself has rightly divided, taught it to us. Be blessed. Or we shall be held accountable for being disobedient as God told Ezekiel he would be if he did not obey God.
God even told Ezekiel speak what I have given you whether the people accept it or reject it. Ezekiel you tell them, you teach them what I have given you to teach my people.

We must obey God and please him always, inspite of rejection or disagreement from others, whether it be other teachers, pastors, friends, family, believers or unbelievers. Amen

Yes, the people Christ is speaking through even today about his grace in these areas are still being rejected by many.

Note: Did you know you can have Grace and still not operate in the Truth of that Grace?

Rejection may come but it is OK, be bold in the Lord, stand for JESUS in love and he will bless you:

★★You don't need man's approval when you have God's approval that you are teaching Truth of his Grace.

God warned his teachers that not all would receive their teachings from God, and he offered them encouragement. The Pharisees did not want to receive the teachings from Paul or Jesus. Many rejected their teaching. Read the following:

John 15: 20-21 Remember the word that I said unto you, the servant is not greater than his lord. If they have persecuted me, they will also persecute you; if they have kept my saying, they will keep yours also. But all these things will they do unto you for my name's sake, because they know not him that sent me.

He has shown us that nothing is new under the Sun. He had to offer encouragement even to the Old Testament Prophets. Read the following.

The following encouragement to Ezekiel

Ezekiel 2:3-10 And he said unto me, Son of man, I send thee to the children of Israel, to a rebellious nation that hath rebelled against me: they and their fathers have transgressed against me: even unto this very day. For they are impudent children and stiff hearted. I do send thee unto them; and thou shalt say unto them, Thus saith the Lord God. And they, whether they will hear, or whether they will forbear, (for they are a rebellious house) yet shall they know that there hath been a prophet among them. And thou, son of man, be not afraid of them, neither be afraid of their words, though briers and thorns be with thee, and thou dost dwell among scorpions: be not afraid of their words, nor be dismayed at their looks, though they be a rebellious house. And thou shalt speak my words unto them, whether they will hear, or whether they will forbear; for they are most rebellious. But thou son of man, hear what I say unto thee; Be not thou rebellious like that rebellious house: open thy mouth, and eat that I give thee. And when I looked, behold, an hand was sent unto me; and lo, a roll of a book was therein; And he spread it before me; and it was written within and without; and there was written therein lamentations, and mourning, and woe.

Ezekiel 3: 7-22 Read Gods encouragement, strength, to Ezekiel about his going forth to speak to the Children of Israel.

We are only God's servants, doing what he has called each of us to do for him.

My goal is to either plant a seed or water a seed, with this moment, for this time span. When I leave I know I would have done as God required me to do, and that he is faithful to bring forth a harvest into your lives as you be obedient to what is being planted and watered in your life today and that will be planted and watered in your life by others from God in the future. Amen. ★★★

1 Cor 3:5-6 After all, who is Apollos? Who is Paul? We are only God's servants through whom you believed the Good News. Each of us did the work the Lord gave us.

In Christ, we are now free from all the curses of the laws, and we now receive all the blessings and promises of the laws by Christ. Now therefore, we are no longer condemned if we walk in the Spirit that comes by Christ.

THINGS I'VE LEARNED

CHAPTER 17

●

QUESTIONS ANSWERED-NOW THAT OUR DISCUSSION OF TITHING AND GIVING IS COMPLETE LET'S ANSWER THE FOLLOWING QUESTIONS

1. **Should I pay tithes by the letter or not?** Since Christ has come you do need to fulfill the tithe through believing in him as Lord in Saviour and receiving his Holy Spirit in your heart. You do not have to keep the carnal ordinances of paying tithes by the letter if you have put your faith in Jesus. You have fulfilled the tithe and offering through Faith and receipt of the Holy Spirit in your hearts. You have fulfilled all the law. Your tithe and offering is with you everyday, everywhere you go. Every time you walk through the door of your church you are bringing the tithe in your heart. You still should have a giving gift in your hand. If you choose to continue to do these things by the letter. Remember that is fine. You are no better or no worse off if you do it by the letter and you are a believer, but you are worse off if you are an unbeliever and think bringing 10% keeps you in right standing.. It must be done by the Spirit. You can give as your giving gift–10%, 1%, 3%, 20%, etc as led by God. As he stirs your heart to give. If you have nothing to give. Bring your praise of thanksgiving to the Lord daily. God will still provide for you and love you.

    God may have you in a Raven by brook season. God is still with you, and will bless you, as his child. The important point is to be a light of his humility through us, under the mighty hand of God in every season.

2. **Is tithing New Covenant as well or Old Covenant? Yes, one fulfilled by the Spirit and the other by the letter of the law.**

3. **Tithing is under the Law but we Live under Grace now, so I do not have to keep tithing by the letter ?** Correct. But you have to fulfill it by the Spirit and you still have to give a gift to the church as led by God.

4. **Don't I need to pay my debts for God said pay those you owe or should I tithe first?** Stop the struggle. Giving is still commanded. Pay your debts and still set aside an amount to give as God stirs your heart, or vice versa. No struggles here.

5. **Don't I need to pay my utility bill and car note for God said take care of your family?** Yes. Again no struggle here anymore.The chains and bondages are off. The curses and condemnations are removed by Christ.

6. **Don't I need to pay my tithes, because you are cursed if you do not pay right?**
No you are not cursed. Christ has come and removed the curse of the law. Tithing is fulfilled by the Spirit, if you are a believer. You cannot be cursed any longer for not paying tithes by the letter.You are only cursed according to the law if you are an unbeliever. Christ became the 100% tithe. Give as God stirs your heart.

7. **What order is correct. How should I prioritize. Should I take care of my household and family by paying my bills 1ˢᵗ and tithes 2ⁿᵈ ? or Should I pay Tithes first and take care of my family 2ⁿᵈ, or is tithing necessary can I just give as I purposed in my heart, because I may not be able to do any giving this week but maybe 30% next week and the week after that maybe only 2%, I'm so confused, I don't want to be cursed?**

Tithing is always priority. Tithing is always first. Putting God First is always priority. The only way to do so is by believing in Christ Jesus, his Son, as your Lord and savior. After receiving Christ as your Lord and Savior, God will be faithful to perform every promise and blessing to us always to take care of our family. Believe in Jesus, give as led by God, and take care of your family. All are required by God without a Curse.

8. **Should I pay tithe on the gross or the net?** Just give as God stirs your heart. There is no more struggle/bondage/curse here,either. Christ has come.

9. **Isn't tithing part of the laws of the land? For God said we are to obey the laws of the land, right?** No tithing has been fulfilled by Christ . It was an ordinance/rule/regulation of the Old covenant.

10. **Do I have to pay a tithe every week. I don't get paid but once per month?** That is fine. Your tithe is fulfilled in you every week. You can give your giving gift when you get paid. Some people get paid weekly, some get paid every 2 weeks, or twice per month, or monthly. Yes, the scriptures tell us to lay aside at the beginning of each week. That is fine. You just will be bringing your weeks in an accumulation at the end of the month. Do not get caught in the legalities of the principle. This is what Jesus corrected the Pharisees on when they were trying to be legalistic with him about healing on the Sabbath and they were rescuing oxen on the Sabbath. He was trying to show them that he was the fulfillment of the Sabbath. He is the fulfillment of the Tithe and offering and Also our giving, but the giving is still required by the letter. He does not want us to get caught up in legalities of his word. He wants obedience to the word. Amen.

Thank God for Christ. Can we see from the above questions how much bondage and struggle and curses we were in trying to live by the laws of tithing and offering by the letter after Christ has come, and we have confessed him as Lord over our lives, and have received his Holy Spirit into our hearts. This is so much bondage and curse. No more, Walk in the newness of the Spirit and mind in Christ Jesus.

THINGS I'VE LEARNED

CHAPTER 18

IN CLOSING

Prayerfully, God has made your way plain. I just believed he knew this was a long and overdue conversation or study that was needed as part of this Journey. Glory to our amazing God for providing this understanding.

Paying tithes and offerings were under the Old Covenant, part of the Old Tabernacle, and fulfilled by Christ, and no longer required to be done by the Letter. However, Giving in any percentage as stirred by God is still commanded. Giving will be in various forms to the church, however giving money still should be one of the forms you use to give to your church home,along with giving of your other resources and time, and gifts and skills. Be also wise and take care of your family then spread it abroad.

Read the scripture on the importance of taking care of your family.

1 Timothy 5:8 But if any provide not for his own, and specially for those of his own house, he hath denied the faith, and is worse than an infidel.

God wanted to make his way plain and give you understanding and set you free in this area, and stop the debate and strife about this area. It may be hard to understand. God knew it. It was back then in biblical days as well on many topics that the apostles and disciples taught with the people

As the following scriptures state:

John 6:60— Many therefore of his disciples, when they had heard *this*, said, This is an hard saying; who can hear it?

Hebrews 5:11-14 thru Hebrews 6:1 Of whom we have many things to say, and hard to be uttered, seeing ye are dull of hearing. For when for the time ye ought to be teachers, ye have need that one teach you again which *be* the first principles of the oracles of God; and are become such as have need of milk, and not of strong meat. For every one that useth milk *is* unskilful in the word of righteousness: for he is a babe. But strong meat belongeth to them that are of full age, *even* those who by reason of use have their senses exercised to discern both good and evil. Therefore leaving the principles of the doctrine of Christ, let us go on unto perfection; not laying again the foundation of repentance from dead works, and of faith toward God

Receive the blessing of God and pray to him to open your eyes and ears as his servant, so you may understand. For he has come through this book to give you his knowledge, wisdom, and understanding and he desires to make it plain to you. Be blessed.

Read the following:

God has come to proclaim liberty, good tiding, understanding, his wisdom and knowledge of him in all things.

Read:
Isaiah 61:1 The Spirit of the Lord GOD *is* upon me; because the LORD hath anointed me to preach good tidings unto the meek; he hath sent me to bind up the brokenhearted, to proclaim liberty to the captives, and the opening of the prison to *them that are* bound.

2 Timothy 2:7 Consider what I say; and the Lord give thee understanding in all things

Proverbs 15:19 The way of the slothful *man is* an hedge of thorns: but the way of the righteous is made plain

We are only God's servants, doing what he has called each of us to do for him.

My goal is to either plant a seed or water a seed, with this moment, for this time span. When I leave I know I would have done as God required me to do, and that he is faithful to bring forth a harvest into your lives as you be obedient to what is being planted and watered in your life today and that will be planted and watered in your life by others from God in the future. Amen. ★★★

1 Cor 3:5-6 After all, who is Apollos? Who is Paul? We are only God's servants through whom you believed the Good News. Each of us did the work the Lord gave us.

THINGS I'VE LEARNED